Painism:
A Modern Morality

Richard D. Ryder

Centaur Press
An imprint of Open Gate Press
London

First published in 2001 by Centaur Press,
an imprint of Open Gate Press
51 Achilles Road, London NW6 1DZ

British Library Cataloguing-in-Publication Programme
A catalogue reference for this book is available from the
British Library.

ISBN: 0 900001 46 1

Printed in Great Britain by
Bell & Bain Ltd., Glasgow

To Emily and Henry – the best!

Dr Richard Ryder is a well-known broadcaster on ethical issues around the world, having appeared on American, Canadian, Australian and Scandinavian television.

In the UK, most recently he has appeared on *The Moral Maze* (Radio 4), *The Heart of the Matter* (BBC2), *The Rise and Rise of Animal Rights* (Channel 4) and *Beastly Business: Power and Propaganda* (BBC2).

Other books include:

Victims of Science: The Use of Animals in Research
(Davis Poynter, 1975 and Centaur Press, 1980).
This book precipitated several debates in Parliament and led to new legislation in Britain and the EU controlling animal experimentation.
'The best informed reference book ever published on the subject.' New Statesman.

Animal Rights – A Symposium (Centaur Press, 1979).
Ryder edited this book based upon the first ever conference on animal rights, held in Cambridge.

Animal Welfare and the Environment (Duckworth, 1992).
The proceedings of the pioneering conference held at Oxford, initiated and edited by Ryder.

Animal Revolution: Changing Attitudes Towards Speciesism
(Basil Blackwell, 1989 and Berg, 2000).
'Ryder has never been afraid to court controversy or to unleash uncomfortable new ideas.' TLS.
'A splendid account.' Peter Singer.

The Political Animal: The Conquest of Speciesism
(McFarland, 1998). *'Full of gems.'*

Contents

Chapter 2: *A New Approach: Painism* 26

Chapter 3: *Some Applications* 66

Acknowledgements

Conversations with friendly philosophers over the years have been of great help to me. The first, way back in Oxford in 1970, after I had proposed my notion of speciesism, was with Stanley and Roslind Godlovitch and John Harris. I also met Gilbert Ryle at this time although I found his discussions of Aristotle entertaining rather than enlightening. Then came Peter Singer whose kind offer of co-authorship of *Animal Liberation* I stupidly turned down; his lucid explanations have helped me many times. Tom Regan, too, has guided me through some of the difficulties of Rights Theory. Later came the good advice of Harvey Green and my other colleagues in the Philosophy Department at Tulane University. Most recently I have been helped by Richard Sorabji, Steve Sapontzis, Heather Evans, Janie Reynolds, Derek Jarrett, Jeannie Cohen, Rupert Woodfin and by Heather Draper. Above all, I thank Dave Robinson for running his highly professional philosophical eye over the typescript. I am grateful to all these and to one of the best natural philosophers I know, my son Henry Ryder, with whom I have been able to discuss the writing of this book. As usual, the really hard work was done by Penny Merrett. I thank them all – and my muse, Louise Woodgate.

Exeter, May 2001

Introduction

I am somewhat nervous about writing an entire book devoted to
ethics and it may seem pretentious to professional philosophers that
I am presuming to do so. I have three excuses. The first is that I
have been thinking about ethics since the age of twelve when I
discovered that my Christian upbringing began to collide with
certain realities. Secondly, having alluded to ethics cautiously in
various publications, I find that some professional philosophers
have been kind enough to take me seriously. Finally, as a psychologist reared in the hard school of behaviourism, I can plead that
it is about time that psychologists such as myself once again
returned to the subject of ethics after a century of neglect.

There are many perennial questions in ethics that have been
discussed for centuries. Among them are: *What are the standards
of right and wrong behaviour? Are these standards objective truths
or are they human inventions? Can they be justified by reason, by
self-interest or in any other way?* I shall address these questions
by providing some new ideas on ethical standards and concluding
that morality is a human invention motivated by our need to have
rules to help us to make decisions, our desire to be consistent and,
above all, by an interaction between reason and our compassion
for others.

From Aristotle onwards, so it seems to me, ethics has been written about in an unnecessarily obscure manner. Personally, I have little patience with those who wrap essentially simple ideas in obfuscation. I have tried to avoid doing so. So, for the sake of clarity, perhaps rather pompously, I have called some of my main conclusions 'rules'. By this I do not want to imply that I demand or expect compliance! My rules are not orders or commands.

There are several new ideas in this book. One is that morality is only about the treatment of *others*. I argue in chapter 1 that Aristotle, and some other writers in antiquity, have profoundly confused the issue by mixing up morality with the provision of psychological advice on how we can enjoy *ourselves*. So I try to sweep away a great deal of traditional teaching on the subject. Another undoubtedly revolutionary idea with which I have been associated for some years is that nonhuman animals should be given a similar moral status to human beings: that what matters morally is the degree of pain and not who or what experiences it. My moral theory of painism which I outline in chapter 2, is also new in that I argue that it is meaningless to aggregate the pains of several individuals when calculating the moral value of an action: each individual is an island when it comes to pain and morality. This rebuts much of conventional ethics. Such innovations have considerable implications for our everyday lives and I examine these in chapter 3. One of these implications is that the severe suffering of one individual is a more serious matter morally than the mild suffering of millions.

We face the new millennium confused about what it is we *should* be doing. With increased scientific knowledge of the universe has come a growing uncertainty about ethics. People now feel the need for a clearly expressed and consistent code by which to live and one based not upon religion. I have attempted to provide such an ethic. I call it *painism*.

Ethics So Far

I want to begin by sketching a brief historical overview of ethics so far. This is a highly personal view and I will use any opportunities that arise to interject my own opinions, sometimes in the form of proposed 'rules'. I will also draw attention to a basic muddle which, I believe, underlies the subject generally.

What is 'morality'? The word itself is ambiguous. It comes from the Latin *mos* (plural *mores*) meaning custom(s) and was translated from the Greek *ethos* (custom) from which the English word 'ethics' is derived. The Oxford English Dictionary defines the adjective 'moral' as:

> 'of or pertaining to the distinction between right and wrong, or good and evil, in relation to actions, volitions or character; ethical.'

Already we can see the source of some confusion. A 'custom' is something which is established – it already exists as a form of behaviour, whereas the 'distinction between right and wrong' is concerned with what *ought* to be. Because an action is customary it does not necessarily mean that it is good. Gang warfare and the torture of enemies, for example, are customary in some parts of the world, but they do not appear to be morally good. The term 'morality', in other words, already incorporates historically the confusion between 'is' and 'ought'. I propose to use both 'ethics' and 'morality' interchangeably to refer only to 'ought' issues. I shall, however, additionally use 'ethics' to mean the *study* of morality.

Sorting out the distinction between 'ought' and 'is', or between values and facts, has taken some centuries. It is now well accepted that factual premises alone cannot imply an 'ought' statement. That is to say it is generally agreed that it is impossible to derive an 'ought' (i.e., morality) only from an 'is' (i.e., the world of facts).

The classical confusion

The most profound confusion, however, and one infrequently remarked upon (if at all), emanates from some of the earliest and most influential writings on the subject of morality. Aristotle (384–322 BC) (at least in translation), often confuses virtuous behaviour with selfish benefit. He blurs the distinction between the self and others. So his *Nicomachean Ethics* is as much a psychological self-help book about how to gain happiness for oneself as it is a book about how we ought to treat *others*. He is chiefly providing advice on how to find 'the good life', specifically through variety, moderation and the use of reason. (Rather vaguely, Aristotle also argues that it is natural for humans to behave morally towards others.)

In my opinion, Aristotle is a great fountainhead of confusion on ethical issues, not least concerning this muddle between what is good for me and what is good for you. The chaos caused by Aristotle continues to bedevil moral debate to this day. I will repeatedly draw attention to this 'classical confusion'. In order to avoid it I propose the following rule:

*Rule 1: Morality is only about the right and wrong treatment of **others**.*

This means that moral discussion is not about how I can gain happiness or success for myself. Such a discussion is a legitimate subject for psychology and psychotherapy, but it is not part of ethics.

One of the greatest influences upon Western ethics has been Thomas Aquinas (*circa* 1225–74). He supported Aristotle's view that everything should fulfil its natural end or purpose (*telos*) and asserted that the Christian religion provides a comprehensive vision of what is both natural (i.e., God's will) and good. This tendency to assert that what is natural must necessarily be good, is still with us, despite the fact that our natural behaviour can cause suffering to others. Certainly, doing what is natural for us to do usually leads to our contentment. I believe that it is only morally good, however, when we help others to achieve such contentment. Too often the ethical debate jumps unwittingly from discussing *my* desires (e.g., to find friendship or truth or – and this is where matters become particularly confusing – to act morally) to the desires of the *moral patient* (e.g., to experience happiness). I believe that the initial emphasis of ethics should be upon the interests and experiences of the victim or moral patient. My innate compassion may or may not spontaneously motivate me to help the victim but this is a matter for psychology. Ethics comes in when I seek to find reasons to support my compassion. In a situation where I feel it is in my interests to harm others, for whom I may feel no compassion, then it is a matter for ethics to produce reasons why I should not harm them. It must remain largely irrelevant to ethics itself whether or not I act morally because I am driven by compassion or by some other motive.

Cultural values

All social cultures contain moral values of some sort. There are, it seems, no human societies that lack values entirely. There can, nevertheless, be considerable differences between the values of one culture and another. In one culture it is considered right to smack naughty children while in another it is considered wrong. Certain forms of behaviour, however, appear to be universally condoned across all cultures. These include, for example, truthfulness and the honouring of promises. So why, in general, are human beings such moral animals? Why, usually, do we want to be good (however goodness happens to be defined in our particular culture)? Surely this is partly, at least, because we all like to have the approval of others. We are programmed genetically to seek social approval. Approval is a most rewarding experience for us, although sometimes it can lead us into trouble. If, for example, we find ourselves in a delinquent gang whose subculture highly values rape and robbery, then there is a strong tendency for us to seek the approval of fellow gang members by raping and robbing. In this instance the gang's idea of what is good is at odds with society's at large. So it seems highly likely that there is an evolutionary advantage for members of our species in behaving in a way that meets with the approval of others; in other words, it is probable that gaining the approval, and hence the cooperation, of others has helped our genes to survive. There is, however, another reason why we are moral animals. Because of the size and complexity of our brains our behaviour is not tied to responding stereotypically to events around us. A particular stimulus may always provoke the same response from an insect but, subjectively at least, as humans we often feel we are faced with a range of possible responses. When we are insulted, for instance, we can either return the insult, lash out physically, plot long-term revenge, smile sweetly or, quite simply, ignore the insult and turn away. Making decisions is never entirely easy. Decision-making itself always involves some anxiety and, on occasions, it can be painful. In order to reduce this intrinsic pain in decision-making we turn to our moral codes to help us. If our moral code tells us it is wrong to respond to an insult with instant physical violence then this is one less option to choose from. In this way the moral code reduces the agony of indecision.

Rule 2: Morality provides us with a framework which facilitates our choice of actions, thus reducing our levels of stress.

Morality and religion

So, where, then, does morality come from? Do we have to invoke the idea of God to answer this question? No. If morality is part of our nature (and probably the nature of some other animals as well) then presumably it has evolved in us. We can speculate that those of our ancestors who possessed morality survived better than those who lacked it, either because they could make decisions faster or because they cooperated better with others, or both.

Why is morality so often bound up with God and religion? We can understand this by considering the main psychological function of religion which is that it attempts to reduce our uncertainties. It does so in three ways, by providing us with *meaning, magic and morality*. In the first place religions attempt to give some *meaning* to the universe around us by explaining how the world came into being and telling us what will happen to us after we die. Then, secondly, through prayer or ritual, religions purport to provide the *magical power* to influence events. Finally, religions provide us with *moral codes* which help us to make decisions and gain the approval of others (including the gods).

It can be seen that science has come a long way towards satisfying two out of three of the psychological needs traditionally satisfied by religion. Science provides, in unprecedented detail, a description of how the world works and it gives us a technology to influence events which far surpasses any of the claims of magic or religion. In other words, science gives us meaning and 'magic' in spadefuls. Science fails, however, to give us a morality. In an age where science has, to an extent, replaced religion, there remains this empty space. In most religions, this moral space is filled with instructions which are allegedly based upon some form of divine authority such as the will of God. Adhering to the moral code is said to gain divine approval while deviating from it risks divine wrath. Over the centuries these have been powerful sanctions but, for many of us today, they carry little weight. But is it still possible to believe in a moral code while not believing in God? Yes, I believe it is. Later, I will explain why I think morality can be based upon compassion and reason alone.

What, however, do the great religions say about morality? Is there any common ground between them? Remarkably, there is. Nearly all of them encourage kindness to others. If we can accept that terms such as 'mercy' and 'love' amount to much the same thing, then we can see that the great religions all urge that we should do to others what we would like to have done to us. Of course, the detail and emphasis differ and in some religions, such as Buddhism, the definition of 'others' includes nonhuman animals, while in Judaeo-Christianity it usually does not. Nevertheless, there is a degree of agreement on the overall moral objectives.

The four languages of ethics

Writers on ethics usually choose one of four 'languages' in which to express their ideas. The first, used by classical ethicists such as Aristotle, talked of *virtues*, admirable traits of character such as justice, wittiness, wisdom, moderation, courage, piety and magnanimity. All virtues were, according to Aristotle, the mid-points or means between the opposing vices of excess and defect; for example, the virtue of courage comes between the defect of cowardice and the excess of foolhardiness. Christians wrote approvingly of charity, patience, purity, humility and benevolence or, as in the case of Thomas Aquinas, of the four cardinal virtues of prudence, justice, fortitude and temperance. The weakness of virtue-language is that it concentrates upon the moral agent and tends to ignore his victim implying, perhaps, that the latter's suffering counts for little provided that his persecutor acts with virtue – for example, with humility or courage.

In the eighteenth century this emphasis upon virtues declined and was replaced by a second language, that was used by the so-called deontologists, who spoke of *duties* and *rights*. Immanuel Kant (1724–1804), for example, argues that we have a duty to follow the moral law even if this is against our inclinations. For Kant, the basic moral requirement for a human being is to be treated as an end in oneself. The concept of rights, both human and animal, also took off in the late eighteenth century.[1] Today, in the writings of philosophers such as John Rawls, Robert Nozick, Ronald Dworkin and Tom Regan, rights-based approaches have been revived.

Some ethicists have used a third language, one that stresses the importance of the *consequences* of actions, supporting, for example, Utilitarianism, the ethical theory advanced by Jeremy Bentham (1748–1832) and John Stuart Mill (1806–73). This proposes that 'actions are right in proportion as they tend to promote happiness, wrong as they tend to produce the reverse of happiness'. Peter Singer is a leading proponent of this school today.

The fourth sort of terminology used is the language of moral *principles* such as democracy, justice, liberty or equality. Like virtue-language, this language has been in use for a long time. Its danger, as we shall see, is that an emphasis upon any one principle tends to reduce the importance of the others.

Having four different moral languages may, at first glance, seem to be very confusing. However, they can all be understood to say much the same thing.

Five bases of ethics

Ethics has been, historically, put upon one of five bases:

(1) Thomas Hobbes (1588–1679) and others have argued that ethics should be based upon a *contractual agreement* between people. The right thing to do is that which could be agreed upon in such a hypothetical contract. David Hume argued against this proposal on the grounds that this contract never actually existed and, furthermore, that the obligation owed to such a contract itself would need a basis.

(2) Traditionally, ethics has been based upon *religion* so that it is described as the following of divine law or the fulfilment of the will of God.

(3) In contrast, *human will* was suggested by Friedrich Nietzsche (1844–1900) as the basis of his own, admittedly odd, morality.

(4) David Hume (1711–76) and others have based ethics upon *sentiment or the passions.* This approach has included the view that ethics is built upon the natural feeling of compassion or sympathy for others.

(5) Immanuel Kant and many others have chosen pure practical *reason* as the fundamental basis of ethics. Classical philosophers such as Aristotle argued that ethics is reason put into practice.

These five bases are not mutually exclusive nor an exhaustive list of possibilities. Later, I will argue that ethics can combine the last two positions, through reason inspired by compassion.

The three levels of ethics

It can be seen that a discussion of ethics takes place at different levels. Sometimes we are discussing theories about ethics itself (this is called *meta-ethics*), sometimes we are concerned with ethical standards or, as it is called, *normative ethics*, and sometimes we descend to an even more practical level as we try to apply those norms and standards to particular problems – this is termed *applied ethics*.

To be fully effective, morality should operate on all three levels. A moral code alone (i.e., normative ethics) without some discussion of its foundations (i.e., meta-ethics) is not likely to be convincing. On the other hand, without some attempt at applying a code to contemporary problems (i.e., applied ethics) it is unlikely to affect behaviour. If one believes that politics and legislation are, ultimately, based upon ethics then politics and the law are themselves powerful forms of applied ethics. Politics is at the cusp where private ethical rules are converted into matters of public law and war.

Rule 3: Politics and the law are applied ethics writ large.

Relativism and universalisability

Following Kant it is sometimes claimed that moral statements are *universalisable*; that is to say that anyone in the same situation ought to act in the same way. It is not right to alter a moral rule for personal reasons nor to make exceptions in one's own favour. Contrasting with this austere approach, although not strictly its opposite, is the idea of moral *relativism* – the notion that moral truth itself is relative to the position of the judging subject. Frequently this argument is used against interference in the customs of different cultures – the suppression, for example, of practices such as cannibalism, circumcision and ritual torture. Increased globalization requires an increased toleration of cultural differences. But are there to be no limits to such toleration? Are there any core values which we consider so important that we should force them upon other ethnic groups? Does it make a moral difference if these ethnic groups have immigrated into our territory? Is it merely a matter of geography? Are these questions to be decided by majority opinion in democracies or can democracies themselves produce immoral 'tyrannies of the majority' over the freedoms of the dissenting individual? How does the concept of human rights, for example, enter into this argument? These are issues we will return to in chapter 3.

Meta-ethics

Meta-ethics examines the meaning of moral terms, psychological issues such as what motivates us to be moral, and more general questions such as whether morality exists independently of human beings.

The meanings of moral terms such as 'good', 'bad', 'right', 'wrong', 'ought' and 'should' are today usually considered to be 'non-propositional' statements. To say 'vivisection is a bad thing' does not seem to reflect the world of fact as firmly as does a statement such as 'vivisection involves the use of animals'. In a world of hard scientific facts morality appears to be a soft entity. Does this mean then that what is right or wrong is merely a matter of culture?

Anthropologists know very well that social customs and values vary considerably from one society to another. As we have seen, moral relativists argue that morality is merely this – a part of traditional culture. Yet, surely, there are two arguments against this. First, that because beliefs can be wrong, so also can be those moral values that are dependent upon such beliefs. For example, a religious belief that human sacrifice is required for the sun to continue to rise every morning, can be shown, scientifically, to be wrong. Yet it might form the basis for certain moral standards, for instance, that it is wicked not to sacrifice humans. If the factual basis for a moral standard can be shown to be wrong, then that moral standard is also likely to be wrong. Secondly, as James Rachels has pointed out,[2] there are some values that are common to all societies, such as the view that it is wrong to murder, to lie and to be neglectful of children.

Moral conclusions are based upon reasons – philosophers call them *premises*. A *valid* moral argument follows rules of logic and is one where the premises support the conclusions. Where the premises themselves are true the argument is said to be not only valid but also a *good* argument. (In deductive argument the conclusions follow from the premises, while in inductive argument we draw inferences from the evidence). With moral arguments there are often two premises, one a *factual premise* and the other a general *moral premise*. For example, if the moral premise is 'causing pain is wrong' and the factual premise is 'keeping pigs in crates causes pain', then the conclusion would be that 'keeping pigs in crates is wrong'. It is usually the moral premise that is contested. But this forms the subject matter of normative ethics which is discussed in chapter 2.

Are moral premises, then, based upon some objective foundation? The confusingly called 'moral realists' argue that this is the case. Some, like Plato, claim that morals, like mathematics, exist outside the mind in an unchanging and universal realm of the forms. Religions have argued that morals are based upon divine authority and so they, too, have placed morality outside of ourselves. Against all this the moral relativists have remained unconvinced and moral sceptics, such as J. L. Mackie,[3] have claimed that a belief in a separate objective realm of ethics is too strange to accept, and that it begs too many questions as to how we can relate to or know of this separate realm.

One must agree that it is easier to comprehend ethics as an artificial human construction. Moral laws are not like the laws of physics, for example. In its normative and applied details, ethics is not a given part of the natural universe. On the other hand, one has to remember that the human mind itself is part of that universe and is the product of its amazing physical laws. So in this indirect sense morality is, indeed, the product of physics and part of the natural world. So we should, I think, adopt a moderate position somewhere between the extremes of moral realism and moral relativism. Such a position, in my view, in no way invalidates ethics. The creation of moral guidelines based upon sound argument remains a highly worthwhile task.

The naturalistic fallacy

It has been argued by G. E. Moore (1873–1958)[4] and others that 'goodness' is not capable of being explained in terms of anything more fundamental. 'Goodness' is like 'yellowness', he argued. To describe 'yellowness' in terms of light of a given wavelength is not to say that the two are identical. Similarly, to describe 'goodness' in terms of pleasure is to make the same mistake; two properties can belong to the same thing without being identical. It is a fallacy, Moore argues, to identify goodness with any natural property; goodness can only be recognised intuitively. (This assertion clearly raises difficult psychological questions about the existence of some special moral sense or moral intuition.) Moore was opposing the Utilitarian view that happiness and goodness are identical. He objected to the conversion of moral terms into factual ones as if by sleight of hand. (Yet, surely, pleasure can be the subjective experience of goodness just as yellowness is the subjective experience of light of a certain wavelength. Did Moore get this confused?)

Morality and selfishness

We can obviously behave morally in order to gain the approval of others or of ourselves, or to avoid punishment. Is moral behaviour, then, inevitably selfish? Thomas Hobbes thought so. He held the cynical view that even our apparently selfless actions are motivated by selfishness. One has to conclude that he is right if 'selfish' is defined to mean that every deliberate action is done because 'I want to do it'. Furthermore, even the sacrificing of my life for another may be motivated by the thought that 'I will not be able to endure my guilt if I do not do so' or, 'I will gain so much approval and fame after my death'. Sometimes such thoughts may hardly, if at all, be conscious but they may still be motivating. Is Hobbes, then, right? Surely we must not confuse the fact that everything I do, even the most unselfish actions, are always motivated by my motives, with the far more doubtful assertion that everything I do is for my benefit. Can I not help others out of a genuine concern for their benefit – either from a sense of duty (as Immanuel Kant asserted) or motivated by my feelings (or 'passions' as David Hume put it)?

Compassion

This is a word that still does not appear in the indices of some very good books on ethics. Strangely, although highly relevant to the central Christian ethic of neighbourly love, compassion as an inherent motive, was not very well addressed by medieval writers and, as a category, it was virtually unknown in Greek thought. Yet the idea of some form of innate goodness in human nature has flickered fitfully over the centuries, often obscured by the 'classical confusion'. Joseph Butler (1692–1752), for example, asserted that we have an inherent capacity for benevolence towards others and he rejected Hobbes' cynical egoism. Like so many writers, however, he muddled morality with psychology by talking simultaneously about what is morally good and what motivates (or is 'good' for) me. The 3rd Earl of Shaftesbury (1671–1713) had similarly argued that we have, by nature, an inclination towards good, which he called 'the moral sense' but again, he confused the argument by saying that the expression of this natural tendency leads to our own personal happiness. Francis Hutcheson (1694–1746) also supported the view that we are immediately pleased by virtuous conduct which promotes the happiness of others. In the nineteenth century the term 'altruism' was invented by Auguste Comte (1798–1857) and used by thinkers such as Herbert Spencer (1820–1903). Arthur Schopenhauer (1788–1860), too, had argued that we have a natural compassion for others and can intuit their sufferings. (Perhaps this is what G. E. Moore meant when he claimed that people know what is meant by the good, and that we have a natural 'moral sense'.)

Marxism overlooked or denied the possibility that humankind has an innate streak of benevolence or compassion. Instead, people were seen as being motivated by their class and economic interests. The influence of Sigmund Freud (1856–1939), whose followers emphasised egoistic sexual, destructive and power motives, further eclipsed the possibility that human beings could also be 'instinctively' benevolent or inherently compassionate towards others. According to most Freudians our conscience (or 'superego') is acquired through upbringing and learning. The influence of Learning Theory and Behaviourism in psychology in the first three-quarters of the twentieth century further enforced the view that behaviour is, firstly, egoistic and, secondly, affected by environmental more than by inherent factors. Drives were postulated for food, water, sex, security, status and for many other rewarding goals, but no altruistic drives, other than parental drives, were seriously considered. At that time little thought was given to the possibility that altruism could have survival value in evolutionary terms.

It was during the widespread reappraisal of the value of interpersonal warmth manifested in the youth movements of the 1960s that it became possible again to consider that people have a naturally kind side. This is now widely accepted. In most human beings, however, the natural sense of compassion for others is constantly being challenged by other feelings such as anger, fear and rivalry. Conventional beliefs, too, such as the idea that one should not 'give in to one's emotions', should keep a 'stiff upper lip', maintain a macho posture and so on, often inhibit the natural flow of compassion. Becoming accustomed to the sight of suffering, or to inflicting it, also dissipates compassion. Related to compassion is squeamishness, a much maligned yet very powerful reaction to the injuries of others that deserves more study and far greater respect. All such feelings are based upon the natural ability to identify with others and to recognise when they may be suffering. In autistic persons this capacity is reduced. In psychopaths it is blocked by anger and resentment. In sadists the contrary feeling – exultation, and even sexual pleasure, occurs at the observation of another's pain; in many people such negative feelings are not far below the surface.

It seems to me that when it comes to ethics, we need to crystallise the actions that we commit when we are being compassionate into a well defined framework of rules, to which we then adhere even when the feeling of compassion itself is absent. Ethical standards are thus inspired by compassion but formalised by reason. Compassion is not the only relevant feeling that develops naturally during childhood. There is also the sense of justice; children are intensely aware of being treated unfairly and seem to quickly comprehend the concepts of equity. We should be able to construct a moral code that goes along very nicely with these two natural currents.

Some other meta-ethics

Much of the ethical argument about what is 'ought' and what is 'is' concerns the classical confusion between ethics and psychology. When I am talking of 'ought' I am talking ethics. When I am discussing what 'is', in terms of what is causing me to behave in certain ways, then I am in the realm of psychology. The ethical argument between the intuitionists, who argue that reason alone can lead us to moral action, and the followers of David Hume who argue that moral actions are driven by emotion (reason being the 'slave of the passions') is also an example of this confusion between ethics and psychology. What drives or pleases me are matters for psychology. Our innate streak of compassion usually (but not always) happens to drive behaviour that is morally right. Very often, however, what is right goes entirely against some of our other drives. A paedophile, for example, might suppress his lust for a child because he considers it to be wrong in principle. This is an example of a drive being suppressed by reason. However, the paedophile's rationality may be supplemented by his sense of compassion which makes him feel that he does not want to do anything to upset the child. Here, we have two drives in conflict – the paedophile's libido and his compassion. The compassion is supported by his reasoned belief that paedophilia is also wrong in principle.

The argument between the moral sense theorists (following Hume) and the intuitionists (believers in the dominant role of reason in ethics) continues to this day. But it is based upon this confusion. The answer to the rather dubious question: 'is morality based on reason or feeling?', is that it can be either and, on occasions, both, as in the case of the cited paedophile. Whether reason itself, without the support of emotion, can drive behaviour is a point to be debated by psychologists although, today, such terms as 'reason' are hardly in vogue in psychology. One drive among many (i.e., compassion) just happens spontaneously to produce behaviour that is usually considered to be morally good. However, moral behaviour more often involves the suppression or control of other drives such as lust, self-assertion or greed. Even compassion itself is sometimes suppressed by certain (misguided) moral principles.

Being too 'soft' on a teenager, for example, is often considered not to be in his best interests in the longer term. Training in the postponement of gratifications or in the endurance of hardships is reckoned to be an investment for greater happiness in the future. More extremely, in the widespread cult of machismo the expression of compassion is often despised and, according to the quasi-ethical code of Nazism, for example, feeling any compassion for certain ethnic groups, far from being considered to be good, was considered to be a failing.

The failure to separate psychology from ethics – or the separation of *what is driving me* from *what I ought to be doing for others* – was a potent source of despair to one of the greatest of all Utilitarian philosophers, Henry Sidgwick (1838–1900). He failed to find any watertight argument to convince egoists of the rationality of universal benevolence. He was right. There is none. There are, however, these two spontaneous tendencies within every human being which usually mitigate the effects of our natural egoism; the first is innate compassion and the second is the need for social approval. The latter is very strong but sometimes (as in the case of an individual who is in a delinquent subculture) it can work the other way by encouraging behaviour that is not benevolent. The former tendency, innate compassion, is, however, present in all of us, as I have argued, although, sometimes inhibited by aggressive attitudes, opposed by other drives, or atrophied by habit or desensitisation.

The answer to all this is, as I have suggested, that we should accept that we tend to act out of self interest. This should not depress Henry Sidgwick or anyone else. (A confusion arises when it is claimed by the so-called *ethical egoist* that we *ought* to act out of self-interest. In my opinion, egoism is not part of ethics. Ethics is only concerned with how we treat others. There is really no such thing as 'ethical egoism'.)

In the first three-quarters of the twentieth century the study of ethics did not seem to advance. Initially G. E. Moore's warnings about the so-called *naturalistic fallacy* scared philosophers away from trying to define 'good' in terms of natural qualities such as pleasure or happiness. Moore and others argued that certain things, such as beauty and friendship, are 'self-evidently' good. Although such *intuitionists* could not agree about what these self-evidently good things are, morality increasingly appeared to be a subjective matter. The French *existentialists*, writing in the aftermath of the horrors of two world wars, seemed to imply that no firm moral standards are possible other than being true to oneself, even if one happens to be a racist or sadist. In Britain, R. M. Hare in the 1950s argued that moral judgements must be 'universalisable'; that is to say, that if I consider a particular action – such as the theft of a diamond ring – to be wrong, then I must also judge any relevantly similar action to be wrong, regardless as to who benefits from it. This was an elaboration of Kant's position. Other British philosophers tentatively began to suggest that, despite Moore's strictures, morality, nevertheless, had to be understood using terms such as 'welfare' or 'flourishing'.

As a psychologist, one has to say at this juncture that many different words can be used to describe what are approximately the same psychological states, for example, 'pleasure', 'happiness', 'welfare' and 'flourishing'. Behaviouristic psychology introduced its own new jargon with terms such as 'reward' and 'reinforcement'. Whereas the philosopher uses the words 'wants' or 'desires' the psychologist tends to say 'drives' or 'motives'. Both, however, have used the word 'preferences'. By concentrating on similarities rather than differences in meaning, ethical arguments can be clarified.

The new field of sociobiology appeared in the 1970s employing its own set of terms but, wading into the field of ethics apparently ignorant of G. E. Moore and David Hume, it sometimes appeared to argue that biological facts (such as evolution) can tell us what we ought to be doing morally. We shall look at this subject later.

Modern normative ethics

American philosophers in the twentieth century may have advanced ethics a little faster than have the Europeans. Thomas Nagel,[5] for example, in 1969 opened a new debate about altruism arguing that reason alone can motivate moral behaviour, for example, in acting to reduce another's pain. R. B. Brandt in 1979[6] proposed that benevolence and honesty can both be rational desires, but that a rational person may support certain moral beliefs and yet not always act in accordance with them. As we will see, John Rawls in 1971 argued that (if we could) we should arrange society as if we were behind 'a veil of ignorance' not knowing what class or race or other category (I have included species) we might be in. In effect this supports Hare's requirements of universalisability.

When, as a schoolboy interested in ethics, I first turned to philosophy, I was bitterly disappointed. Instead of enlightenment all I found was something called Logical Positivism – a preoccupation with the analysis of language. So I resolved to try to think things out for myself. The social conventions of the 1950s were rigid and so were the rules of respectable behaviour. The 1960s generation challenged this respectability, questioning and often defying society's conventions on sexual behaviour and the acceptance of authority. It seemed to many of us at the time that society had the wrong priorities – a preoccupation with class status, a reverence for orthodoxy and the ideals of patriotism and masculinity. The decade of the 1950s had been a hangover from the years of the Second World War. Military values still permeated a drab society. Toughness, obedience and self-discipline were the order of the day. Cars were mostly black and clothes were mostly grey – grey flannel trousers, grey knitted pullovers and grey jackets. Ideas on morality were also grey and were largely restricted to a puritanical disapproval of sexual behaviour outside marriage. The subject of sex was so surrounded by guilt and secrecy that at the age of twelve I still did not know how babies were born. Yet, somewhere in my Christian upbringing I had learnt of a merciful Jesus who had, apparently, shown no obsession with sexual purity. Instead, he had taught that we should 'love our neighbours' – a strange phrase that took me some years to understand. (It would have been better if the Bible had said – 'show compassion for others'.) The daily injunctions I received to 'be good' and to 'behave properly', however, seemed to have little connection with Jesus. They were somehow related to respectability, decency and to demonstrating one's class position. Out of all this confusion I eventually formulated my own ethical standards based upon what I subsequently learned was called the

Golden Rule – doing to others what I would like them to do to me.

Today, the decade of the 1960s is often maligned, especially by traditionalists. Yet it was largely about a search for a new morality. It rejected the claim that sex is the most crucial moral issue and began to question the morality of war, the work ethic and the atom bomb. Racism and sexism were also challenged. In 1970, I added the idea of speciesism to the list of morally suspect attitudes[7] and the ensuing animal liberation movement went on to play a significant part in reviving the subject of ethics itself through the writings of Peter Singer, Tom Regan and others.

The first three-quarters of the twentieth century were riven with war and suffering. Yet, despite these ethically challenging events, little of significance had been published in the field of ethics since G. E. Moore's *Principia Ethica* in 1903. W. D. Ross, however, consistent with the militaristic culture of the times, had published in the 1930s his view that ethics was about *duties*. Ross's list of 'self-evident' duties included justice, gratitude, fidelity, self-improvement, reparation, beneficence and non-maleficence. When several duties are in conflict, Ross argued, we should intuitively give precedence to the weightiest. (How this judgement of weight is to be made remains something of a mystery.) The last three decades of the twentieth century saw significant progress in ethics. On the normative level there have been (including the work of the anti-speciesists) four major areas of interest, represented, for example, in the writings of John Rawls, Ayn Rand, the Rights Theorists and the new Utilitarians.

John Rawls

In 1971 John Rawls published his *Theory of Justice*. In this book he defends his idea of 'justice as fairness' as an alternative to Utilitarianism. A just society, Rawls argues, upholds individual liberty and is designed to raise the welfare of its worst-off members (see chapter 3). Rawls said that society should be arranged as if we are behind a 'veil of ignorance' and did not know what our own position in society, wealth, gender, role or abilities would be. We would, said Rawls, insist, first, on everyone having the maximum liberty compatible with others' liberty and, secondly, that wealth be distributed in order to make the worst off members of society as well off as possible. This latter requirement has been called the *maximin principle* because it seeks to maximise the benefits of those living at the minimum level in society. Rawls' position can be criticised by psychologists such as myself for not providing evidence that people really would behave in such a way and would not, for example, prefer to maximise average welfare, thus giving themselves a greater chance of higher benefits, despite the greater risk of destitution. Some people, after all, are inveterate gamblers and like to take risks of this sort.

Ayn Rand

The writings of Ayn Rand[8] for a while revived an interest in so-called ethical egoism which proposes that we should each consider only our own interests. Rand extolled selfishness and individual achievement but was forced to concede that 'true' self interest is not always served by cheating, stealing or by other anti-social behaviours. In my opinion the discussion of what we need for ourselves is not, per se, a part of ethics. As I have asserted, ethics is, by definition, about how we treat *others*. Only when selfishness has implications about how we treat others is it an ethical issue. *Surely, it is altruism and not selfishness that is the essence of morality.*

The new Rights Theorists

Talk of 'rights' goes back at least to John Locke (1632–1704) in the seventeenth century. In the eighteenth century the idea of rights became a part of revolutionary thought in France and America. The concept was, however, partially eclipsed in the following centuries by Utilitarianism and Marxism. Locke listed three human rights: to life, liberty and property. The American Declaration of Independence in 1776 substituted 'happiness' for 'property'. Generally, talk of 'rights' rather than 'duties' is the language of the oppressed. It is victims or moral patients, or those who plead on their behalf, who naturally slip into rights-talk. The language of duties tends to be that of the powerful, of those who can control events. Moral rights should not be confused with legal rights although, as laws proliferate, what were once moral rights may become enshrined in law, and thus become legal rights. A distinction ought also to be made between a right to do something (an active right) and a right to have something done to one (a passive right). Although talk of rights is, for historical reasons, not favoured among many British philosophers it is, as Brenda Almond points out,[9] regarded as valid in most societies in the world today. Conventions on human rights are recognised in international law and there is much interest in extending rights to nonhuman animals. Who, then, can have rights? Various categories have been suggested – living things, sentient or conscious things, those who can reason or those who can choose. Rights will sometimes conflict with other rights and various rules of priority have been suggested. Rights, if they apply to everyone equally, tend to put a protective fence around individuals so that the interests of the majority (as in Utilitarianism) do not so easily overrule the rights of the individual. For example, however many people may benefit from her will, it is still quite wrong to murder Aunt Agnes; she is said to have an absolute right (or nearly so) not to be killed against her wishes.

Opposition to the idea of rights comes from both the political Right and Left. The Right suspects that rights-talk is a demand that yet more taxpayers' money be handed over to the disadvantaged or 'incompetent' members of society. Morality, says the Right, should be a question of duties and not of rights. Misquoting Hobbes, the fallacy is often reiterated that in order to have rights one must be able to observe duties (thus, at a sweep, denying rights to infants, the severely disabled and many invalids). On the Left, however, the Marxists also oppose the notion of rights because Marxism perceives morality generally as ivory tower speculation and a form of bourgeois special pleading that gets in the way of the class struggle. Moreover, Marxism sees the idea of individual rights as a threat to the power of the state. (It is, however, this *individualism* of Rights Theory that is, in my opinion, one of its most attractive features, *see* chapter 2.)

In the twentieth century attempts were made to make rights the foundation for ethical theory. Robert Nozick,[10] for example, argued that we have absolute rights to liberty, life and (legitimately acquired) property and Ronald Dworkin[11] founded his theory upon a basic right to equal concern and respect, and advocated intervention by the state to protect rights.

Such Rights Theories are *rule-based* and so reject *consequentialist* theories such as Utilitarianism which judge actions to be right or wrong on the basis of their consequences alone. Often the two sorts of theories overlap in practice. For example, if Johnnie murders Aunt Agnes then this killing is likely to be wrong according to both types of theory. However, if the consequences of killing Aunt Agnes are that a hundred other lives are saved then, according to some consequentialists, her murder could be justified. Consequentialism has a flexibility that Rights Theories can lack. Utilitarianism is the leading example of consequentialism.

The new Utilitarians

Utilitarianism can be divided into sub-types, such as *act Utilitarianism* and *rule Utilitarianism*. According to act Utilitarianism it is the consequences of the particular act that count when judging whether it is right or wrong. The main difficulty with this approach is that, in practice, it is often extremely difficult and time-consuming to try to calculate the consequences of an action. If one is trying to calculate in advance of an act then it is doubly difficult. Indeed, strictly speaking, it is impossible to predict consequences with certainty – the Earth, for example, may be obliterated by an asteroid or by some other unexpected cosmic event before all the consequences of an action can occur. Anyway, ordinary human society itself is extremely unpredictable – and even benevolent actions may turn out to have unintended bad consequences in the long term. Rule Utilitarianism gets round some of the problem by laying down rules, the following of which has been generally found to lead to the best consequences. Right actions are those which conform to these rules. The problem with this approach is that circumstances can change. Rules are not always the best way to deal with changing circumstances or unusual cases. A hybrid approach may be, in practice, the best.

Rule 4: Stick to ethical rules unless you have the time and information necessary to calculate (as certainly as possible) the exact consequences of an action, or you have good reason to believe that circumstances are new or unusual.

On occasions, rule Utilitarianism has been applied to prevent the occurrence of the apparently shocking implications of act Utilitarianism. Today, however, rule Utilitarianism in its pure form has little support and most philosophers regard it with disfavour.

What is called *classical* or *hedonistic Utilitarianism* is that which endeavours to maximise happiness or pleasure. As J. S. Mill stated, 'actions are right in proportion as they tend to promote happiness, wrong as they tend to produce the reverse of happiness'. Peter Singer has defined classical Utilitarianism as holding:

> that every action is to be judged good or bad according to whether its consequences do more than any alternative action to increase – or, if that is impossible, to limit any unavoidable decrease in – the net balance of pleasure over pain in the universe.[12]

In the twentieth century R. M. Hare proposed that universalisable judgements must prescribe what is most in agreement with the preferences of all those affected by an action. What is called *preference Utilitarianism* stipulates that the rightness of an action depends upon its satisfaction of people's preferences. Preference is not quite the same as happiness, pleasure or pain. Its advantages, as a concept, appear to the psychologist to be that preference behaviour (i.e., whether or not a subject chooses one thing rather than another) can be directly observed whereas the subjective states of others (such as happiness) cannot be so perceived. Also, 'preference' covers both pleasurable and painful experiences. Furthermore, preference behaviour can easily accommodate the masochist who, in certain circumstances, derives a pleasure from experiencing pain that is greater than that pain.

Peter Singer is, perhaps, the best known of all modern Utilitarians. He has played a major role not only in reviving Utilitarianism but Applied Ethics itself. Before Singer, ethics was largely regarded as an abstruse field which had little to say about every-day living. In the twenty-first century, however, it is a subject taught in almost every university and college. The clarity of Singer's writing and his mastery of all aspects of the subject have made ethics accessible to the ordinary reader in a way not pre-viously achieved by most philosophers. Singer admits that he is best known for his book *Animal Liberation*,[13] first published in 1975, in which he backed the new Oxford-based pro-animal move-ment by supporting our claim that species is as irrelevant to moral status as is race or gender. He used my term *speciesism* to attack the exploitation of animals in laboratories, intensive farms and elsewhere. In his *Practical Ethics* of 1979[14] Singer covers a number of contemporary issues such as abortion, euthanasia, poverty and the environment, approaching each 'by seeking the solution that has the best consequences for all affected.' Singer describes himself as a preference Utilitarian, understanding 'best consequences' as 'that which satisfies the most preferences weighted in accordance with the strength of the preferences'.[15] His questioning of the sanc-tity of human life, especially as regards the proposed killing of severely disabled neonates, has caused considerable controversy. Less contentious has been his support for abortion and his view that wealth should be shared with those in desperate need. We will look further at such issues in chapter 3.

Conclusions

I hope this idiosyncratic overview of ethics has demonstrated at least one thing – that the subject is not yet agreed. I have suggested that morality helps us to gain social approval and to make deci-sions. Yet ethics operates on many different levels and there are still many unanswered questions and unsolved problems. My own further suggestions as to solutions will follow next. In this chapter I have also emphasised the need to avoid the classical confusion, as I have called it, by distinguishing between the psychological question, 'what is good for me?', and the ethical question, 'how can I be good to others?'

A New Approach: Painism

In the last chapter I made the distinction between the psychological and ethical approaches arguing that the latter concerns only our treatment of *others*. If we can agree that the ultimate criteria of what is morally good and bad are happiness and suffering, respectively, then psychology will continue to play a key role in ethics by helping us to ascertain what makes others to be happy and to suffer – and how I can increase others' happiness and reduce their suffering. In this chapter I expound my own theory of ethics.

Painism

Painism is a term I coined in 1990 to describe the theory that moral value is based upon the individual's experience of pain and that pain itself is the only evil. I use *painient* and *painism* to denote, respectively, endowment with the capacity to feel pain (and those possessing this capacity) and the principle that the moral code should be based upon this capacity. I interpret pain broadly to include all negative experiences, that is to say, all forms of suffering, mental as well as 'physical'. So the words 'pain' and 'suffering', as I use them, are interchangeable.

I consider that other great moral objectives such as liberty, justice, equality, and fraternity are important only because it is believed (often correctly) that they reduce suffering. For example, why do people want justice? Because it will make them feel less aggrieved; it will reduce their pain. Why do they want liberty and equality? Because they believe these conditions will reduce their sufferings.

Rule 5: Pain (i.e., suffering) is the only evil.

Rule 6: The moral objective is to reduce the pains of others.

Rule 7: All aims and ideals such as justice, democracy, peace, equality and liberty are good only as means toward this end: they are believed to reduce pain.

Pains cannot be aggregated across individuals

I reject the aggregation of pains and pleasures across individuals that is a central feature of other systems of ethics such as Utilitarianism. This is one of the key features of painism.

Utilitarianism will justify torture if the sum total of benefits caused to several others is considered to be greater than the pain inflicted. The gang rape of a woman, for instance, can be justified if the aggregated pleasures of all the rapists exceeds her suffering. This must be wrong. Around each individual is the boundary of its own consciousness and so such aggregations of pains and pleasures across individuals make no sense. Consciousness does not cross the boundary between one individual and another, so neither can meaningful calculations of pain. There exists a barrier between individuals through which consciousness cannot pass. However much I empathise or sympathise with your pain I never actually feel that same pain. For each individual only his or her pain is real. The pains of others are merely reports of pain, or the husks of pain. The pain of A is as different from the pain of B as is a piece of chalk from a lump of cheese. So, if there are a hundred people each suffering X amount of pain, the significant pain score is X, and not 100X. If there is one painient suffering 10 units of pain and one suffering 5 units of pain, the meaningful pain score is 10, not the sum total of 15. In other words, *the morally significant* *measure of pain in a group of painients is the **maximum** felt by any **one** of them. I conclude, therefore, that the moral priority is to try to reduce the pain of the maximum sufferer in each case.*

I am aware that this point of view flies in the face of orthodoxy and has considerable practical consequences for ethical living. Nevertheless, I feel sure I am right! Only if it became possible to link brain to brain directly so that the sufferings of several individuals became experienced by all of them might we be required to aggregate their sufferings for ethical purposes.

Two points need to be added here. First, that although it is meaningless to aggregate pains and pleasures across individuals it is perfectly possible to do so within the same individual. We are all experiencing a mixture of pains and pleasures most of the time. I can enjoy writing while suffering from a slight headache. At the same time, I may be suffering from the painful thought, at the back of my mind, that I must arrange to visit my dentist while also enjoying the sensation of warm sunshine falling on my back. Negative and positive ideas, emotions and sensations all can be aggregated to describe my overall algesic state. Secondly, it can be seen that one of the most obvious consequences of not permitting the aggregation of pains and pleasures across individuals is that the number of individuals affected by an action becomes irrelevant. One can no longer argue that action Y is better than action Z because more individual painients benefit from Y than from Z. *If there is a choice between protecting many from mild pain or reducing the severe pain of just one individual then the latter course should be taken.* As painists we are primarily concerned about maximum sufferers. Killing 100 people painlessly becomes less wrong than torturing one of them to death. It is customary, but wrong, to measure the moral importance of disasters (plane crashes, acts of terrorism and so on) by the number of people who are killed or injured. Instead, we should be asking, 'how much pain was experienced by the individual who suffered most?' Weapons of mass destruction are no worse, morally speaking, than are bows and arrows.

Rule 8: The quantity of pain suffered by the maximum sufferer matters far more than the quantity of individuals affected.

Our main concern, then, is with the individual, A, who is suffering the most pain. We should try to reduce her pain. When the level of her pain reaches that of the next highest sufferer B our primary concern should switch to B and so on. This does not mean that we should be bothered only by the pains of A and B. If we can, at the same time, reduce the pains of lesser sufferers, C and D, then we should do so, provided that our efforts for them do not impede our pain-reducing work for A and B. If our analgesic efforts on A's behalf are, for some reason, totally ineffective, then, of course, we should switch our attentions to B, C and D. It may well be that A is beyond our reach whereas C and D are easy to assist.

When I was asked by Peter Singer to produce some ethical rules of thumb for concerned animal experimenters I formulated them as follows.[1]

Rule 9: Speciesism is always wrong.

Speciesism is similar to racism, ageism and sexism. Pain is pain regardless of the species of the sufferer. We should always bear this in mind. (Remember that 'pain' here covers all forms of suffering including fear, boredom and distress.) Try to act, therefore, as though human interests count for no more than nonhuman interests.

It follows that all my moral rules can be applied in the everyday treatment of humans as well as of nonhumans.

*Rule 10: The aggregation of pains and pleasures across
individuals is meaningless.*

Consciousness, and hence painience, is bounded by the boundaries of the individual. It is wrong, therefore, to try to justify inflicting pain on any individual by aggregating the supposed or actual benefits accruing to several others. Try to act as though the interests of the many count for no more than the interests of one.

*Rule 11: Our first moral concern should always be with the
individual who is the maximum sufferer.*

It is not the total number of individuals suffering that matters morally. It is the degree of their sufferings that is of concern. In particular, as a priority, we should try to help the ones who suffer most, the maximum sufferers. When their pains are reduced there will be new maximum sufferers to attend to, and so on. So try not so much to reduce the quantity of individuals affected as to reduce the severity of the pain experienced by every one of them.

Rule 12: It is always wrong to cause pain to A merely in order to increase the pleasure of B.

It is wrong, therefore, to rape. It is also wrong to perform painful research that is merely for career advantage, convenience, or luxury; tests on animals of non-medical cosmetics are an example. Whatever the amount of pleasure gained from such products, these experiments are wrong and should not be performed. No amount of pleasure gained justifies the causing of *any* pain. Do not, therefore, carry out even mildly painful procedures for trivial purposes. (On pp. 53–4 and 122–3 I make a distinction between 'indirect' pleasures caused by drive-reduction and 'direct' pleasures such as listening to music. It is only the latter that are affected by this Rule.)

Rule 13: Only if there are no alternatives may causing (unconsented to) pain to A be allowed.

Causing even mild pain or discomfort is, of course, always quite wrong (regardless of benefit) if there are other less painful ways of achieving the same results. These should always be tried first.

Rule 14: The pain to be reduced must always be severe.

We should only cause pain to A (in order to help B) if B's pain is severe. In other words, it is legitimate to hurt A only if B's predicament is extreme.

Rule 15: The action must be likely to succeed.

We do not want to cause pain to A and then discover that this action does nothing to help B. We should first carefully review the probabilities of pain and benefit arising from our actions.

Rule 16: Whatever the benefits, it is always wrong deliberately to cause pain that is severe or prolonged. So, regardless of benefits, torture is always wrong.

Of course, such rules of thumb can always be challenged on theoretical grounds but decision-makers need guidelines to help them in the here and now.

Notice that I have suggested that the severity of pain should be judged according to both its *intensity* and its *duration*. Perhaps a short intense pain is as bad as a prolonged lesser pain. We do not habituate well to pain. Pains that are chronic continue to be bothersome. Research could be done to discover whether people dislike short and intense pain less than prolonged but less intense pain. I predict that considerable individual differences, based upon personality, would be found. The moral badness of any particular pain depends upon the preferences of each individual. Short intense pains will be a greater evil for individual A, whereas individual B will find prolonged lesser pain the greater evil. Ultimately, we are concerned with the preferences of the individual. Here we enter a psychological and semantic minefield – if A prefers one sort of pain and B prefers another, then do they each experience pains in the same way?

Ultimately, we are interested, surely, in the *total experience* of the individual and thus in their preferences. Strictly speaking, we ought to ascertain the pain preferences of individuals before making moral decisions. We are not concerned about objective measures such as the voltage of an electric shock, nor its duration in seconds – we are, instead, concerned as ethicists only in the subjective experience of that shock; the unpleasantness of the experience. The only way we can infer this is from the behaviour (including verbal behaviour) of the sufferer. (Direct readings from the brain may one day prove to correlate exactly with the subjective experience of pain. That will make our job, as ethicists, far easier.)

Research by Patrick Wall, Ron Melzack and others has found that people describe sensory pain along some seven dimensions. For example, pains are described as *punctate* (pricking, boring, stabbing), *incisive* (sharp or cutting), *constrictive* (pinching, gnawing, crushing), *tractive* (tugging, pulling, wrenching), *thermal* (hot, burning, scalding), *dull* (sore or aching), or by some other sensory or pseudo-sensory terms such as *tingling* or *stinging*. People also use temporal or rhythmic terms to describe sensory pain (flickering, quivering, pulsing, throbbing, beating, pounding, jumping, flashing or shooting) which mostly suggest that pain is commonly experienced as being rapidly discontinuous or fluctuating in some way. Melzack has found that pain is also described in terms that are less sensory than *affective* – tiring, sickening, suffocating, terrifying, gruelling or wretched. (These affective aspects of sensory pain are reactions to the pain. He is not describing the painful emotions themselves.) Most usefully for ethicists he has also described, and rated on a scale of 5, terms commonly used which he considers to be evaluative, ranging e.g., from *mild* (rated 1), annoying, discomforting and troublesome to miserable, *distressing* (rated 3), intense, horrible, unbearable and *excruciating* (rated 5).[2] Is it, then, proper to combine the intensity and duration of pains in some way if it is really pain-preference that we need for ethical calculations? Strictly speaking, it is not. But unless we can measure individual pain-preferences (verbally or in terms of avoidance behaviour, for example), then it seems a useful second best approach.

Consciousness

Consciousness is of central importance to painism. I see consciousness as an emergent property of the individual brain, being anchored to it. The individuality of consciousness is one of its strangest attributes. The question 'why is my consciousness mine?' remains unanswered. Millions of other brains very similar to mine exist or have existed. Why was 'I' never present in any of those brains? Does this sense of 'me-ness' arise solely from the memories stored within my brain? No, because even amnesics can have sensations that they feel are 'theirs'. However, some of those who have suffered brain damage can partially lose this sense of identity – denying, for example, that some of their limbs belong to them. It is hard to reconcile the individuality of consciousness with the persuasive view of those physicists who argue that the natural world is inter-connected by *fields* that unify apparently distinct entities. Con-sciousness, however, is a matter for individuals; we are not aware of being part of any field of consciousness (*pace* Carl Jung). The individual character of consciousness underlines the ethical impor-tance of each individual and reinforces my view that the pains of several individuals cannot meaningfully be aggregated.

During the 1990s many scientists and philosophers published on the subject of consciousness. None, however, managed to pro-vide a satisfactory answer to the question, 'how does the brain produce consciousness?' Convinced that only an extraordinary theory can account for such an extraordinary phenomenon some claimed that consciousness is as fundamental as time or space and others began to use quantum mechanics to try to find a solution to the problem. It should, I think, be pointed out that both relativity and quantum theories – the two revolutionary theories of modern physics – rely upon something rather similar to consciousness. In relativity theory the position of an observer, for example, will affect time recorded on a moving clock. But, surely, in this context, 'observation' can be understood to be synonymous with 'conscious-ness'. Even more strikingly, the so-called Copenhagen interpre-tation used in quantum theory postulates that quantum systems are in superposed states that are only determined *when they are obser-ved or measured*. Therefore, is it not possible that consciousness plays a fundamental role in the physics of the universe? For exam-ple, elementary particles sometimes appear to spring into existence as real objects only when they are *observed*. I think it is still too early to be sure whether consciousness has this creative role. What, for example, happened in the universe before complex life (and presumably consciousness) had evolved? Were there other forms of consciousness? Consciousness is certainly a remarkable thing and its mechanism is not understood. We are like Stone Age people confronted with television and the apparent miracle as to how a black box with wires to the wall can produce talking heads. Emer-gence, as demonstrated, for example, by television, is nearly always the effect of scale. In close-up, things look quite different than from

33

a distance. Something as simple as scale, very strangely, also plays a part in determining whether or not the complex laws of quantum theory apply. Brains function at a scale where both quantum and classical physics appear to operate – they are on the cusp.

Painism supersedes sentientism

The theory of painism was developed as an attempt to reconcile aspects of Utilitarianism (viz., its emphasis upon pain) with the Rights tradition (viz., its emphasis upon the supreme importance of the individual). As the creator of the term *speciesism* I am not, of course, speciesist in my use of the word *individual*; this refers to any imaginable painient thing – human, nonhuman, biological, mechanical, terrestrial or alien. Pain is pain regardless as to who or what experiences it. If, one day, conscious and painient machines are produced then they, too, will become morally considerable.

The theory of painism has emerged from what was sometimes previously termed *sentientism*. Andrew Linzey and I used this term in the 1970s. John Rodman attacked it on the grounds that it established too narrow a moral circle. Eventually I rejected *sentientism* in favour of *painism* on three grounds:

(1) that sentientism might be deemed to refer to *any* sort of feeling or sensation – or even to sentient beings incapable of experiencing pain at all. (Alien life forms on other planets, for example, may have evolved systems for the avoidance of danger which do not include the subjective experiences of pain.)

(2) that *sentientism* and *sentient* were words not popularly understood whereas *painism* and *painient* could be easily grasped and thus be of greater use in applied ethics, and

(3) that these words usefully fill some significant gaps in the English language.

The Belgian philosopher Johan Braeckman has used the term *pathocentrism* in rather the same sense, although the Greek word *pathos* (from which *pathocentrism* presumably is derived) is rather wide in its meaning as it covers not only suffering but also disease and emotion (some of which may not be painful at all).

Pain

What do I mean by *pain*? I mean everything that is a negative experience. Distress, fear, shame, grief, irritation, boredom, envy and every other form of suffering, including all 'bodily' pains, from blisters to bunions. I believe all experiences are tinged with either pain or pleasure and that none are entirely neutral. Some emotions (such as fear and grief) are painful while others, such as joy, are pleasant. Some, such as anger, may be both painful and pain-reducing. Sensations and perceptions can also be understood to have painful qualities. Pain (suffering) is not itself an emotion nor a sensation. The two great moods – *depression* and its opposite (which strangely has no common name save *euphoria* although its clinical extreme is *mania*) are the epitomes of pain and pleasure and colour all experiences. Sooner or later, brain research will show that all pleasures, however different their causes, from Beethoven to baseball, will share some common cerebral mechanism. The same will be said of all varieties of pain.

Jeremy Bentham rightly lumped together all positive and negative experiences in his principle of Utility:

> By utility is meant that property of any object, whereby it tends to produce benefit, advantage, pleasure, good, or happiness (all this in the present case comes to the same thing) or (what comes again to the same thing) to prevent the happening of mischief, pain, evil, or unhappiness to the party whose interest is considered.[3]

Why is pain bad?

Another problem for painism is also shared by other theories. On what is its moral premise based? In the case of painism, why is pain considered to be bad? I believe the answer is circular. Morality is about good and bad and in one definition 'bad' simply means painful. Pain itself is always bad even if, *indirectly*, it may lead to benefits. Always we return ultimately to the conscious experience of pain. The lives of all painient creatures are dominated by the twin experiences of pleasure and pain, of reward and punishment, of positive and negative stimuli.

These are the two great principles which shape our lives and underlie all the main theories of psychology from Freud to Skinner and to the present day. Morality derives from this fact. What is it that good things have in common? They all give pleasure. What property is it that all bad things share? They all cause pain (in its broad sense). Killing, lying, cheating and stealing are bad because they cause pain to others. Injustice, inequality, the lack of liberty and the absence of beauty are bad because they, too, cause pain. Neglecting and rejecting are bad for the same reason. Pain is the common feature of all bad things. A bad thing is that which causes pain.

Aristotle said that people pursue pleasure, honour and understanding because they believe that they will find happiness by doing so. However, he also said that nobody pursues happiness for the sake of finding something else. I believe, similarly, that nobody avoids pain in order to avoid anything else but pain.

Some readers may feel puzzled that I emphasise pain rather than pleasure. I admit that I do see these two basic experiences (provided both are defined in their broadest meanings) as superficially opposite ends of the same dimension. Of course, one can experience simultaneously several different sorts of pains and pleasures. Although it does not make sense to aggregate the pains and pleasures of several individuals it can be quite proper to do so within the same individual. But I have chosen to concentrate upon pain rather than pleasure for the reason that the avoidance of extreme pain matters more to us than the achievement of extreme pleasure. *At its extreme, pain is more powerful than pleasure can ever be.* Pain spoils pleasure more surely than pleasure distracts from pain. Admittedly, this is a matter of psychology and not ethics. But it does remain important for applied ethics that pain overrules pleasure within the individual far more effectively than pleasure can dominate pain. Recent research in economics supports this asymmetric nature of pain and pleasure. Daniel Kahneman and Amos Tversky have found that people are 'loss averse', getting greater negative utility from losing £100 than positive utility from gaining it.[4] Steven Pinker makes a similar point:

There are twice as many negative emotions (fear, grief, anxiety, and so on) as positive ones, and losses are more keenly felt than equivalent gains. The tennis star Jimmy Connors once summed up the human condition: 'I hate to lose more than I like to win.' The asymmetry has been confirmed in the lab by showing that people will take a bigger gamble to avoid a sure loss than to improve on a sure gain, and by showing that people's mood plummets more when imagining a loss in their lives (for example, in course grades, or in relationships with the opposite sex) than it rises when imagining an equivalent gain.[5]

So does not direct pleasure matter, morally? It does. Consider a group of well-fed but unhappy children who are taken to a pantomime. At the interval, all of them are observed to be smiling happily. There are, no longer, any discernible maximum sufferers. Does one's moral duty towards them end at that moment? No, there remains a duty, albeit a far weaker duty, to make them happier still. The ice-cream lady beckons.

However, in my view, pain is more powerful than pleasure morally as well as psychologically. Consider the case of the rapist or sadist whose pleasure is even greater than his victim's pain. Are his actions thereby justified? Of course not. The extreme pleasure of A can never justify the infliction of even mild pain on B. So, for painists the primary duty is to alleviate pain, specifically the pain of the greatest sufferers. Only when this is done should attention be turned to the enhancement of happiness through increasing direct pleasures.

Rights and duties

Roger Scruton and others have attacked painism on the grounds that it is allied to Rights Theory.[6] As I have already said, I consider that *rights* are a human creation and that we bestow them upon others. Rights do not exist on their own. The concept of duty is a similar human invention. Some people like to use the word duty and some prefer the word rights. This depends upon their psychology. Duties and rights are, in my opinion, opposite sides of the same coin. When I speak of rights I am normally speaking of passive moral rights and, principally, the right not to be deliberately subjected to pain. In practice, ethical decisions are based upon degrees of suffering. Therefore, as individuals differ in what hurts them, rights will differ between individuals and, quite markedly, between individuals of different species. Humans, for example, suffer if denied the right to vote in elections – so this is important for humans but it is not important for other species. Access to eucalyptus leaves is, however, very important for koalas and so the right of access to eucalyptus leaves is an important right for them. Rights – if one wishes to use this term – should be linked to pain rather than to specific actions or events. A 'right to vote' matters a great deal for humans but is meaningless in the case of koalas. Pain, however, matters a great deal to all of us.

Scruton is one of the small number of modern philosophers who has tried to argue that animals lack moral status (or rights) because they cannot observe duties. Lacking the ability to observe duties is, of course, a characteristic also of infants and some severely ill or handicapped human adults. Are these individuals also to be denied rights? Surely, the weak are particularly needful of protection. Children and animals are alike in this respect. Similar attempts to strip animals of moral standing have been made by claiming that they lack other qualities such as self-consciousness, autonomy or the capacity for abstract thought. Surely these are morally irrelevant qualities. Painience is all that matters morally.

Trade-offs

The aggregation of the pains and pleasures of several individuals is not the same as saying that the pain of A can be justified by the reduction of pain in B. Aggregations and trade-offs are not the same. I believe that you cannot meaningfully add up or aggregate the pains and pleasures of *several* individuals, but this is not the same as saying that the pains of one individual cannot be justified by or traded off against the benefits to another single individual. Imagine, for example, causing mild inconvenience to individual A in order to reduce the extreme agony of B. Is not this justified? Imagine you see a very heavy man unwittingly sitting upon a child, causing that child intense pain as bones and organs are damaged and broken. For the sake of argument we shall say that the fat man is brain-damaged and so does not even realise what he is doing. Are you not justified in giving the man a gentle shove, causing him trivial inconvenience as he topples sideways? Common sense suggests that you are. Yet here we are deliberately causing slight suffering to an innocent individual in order to save a child from agony. In other words, we are prepared, quite rightly, to trade off the little pain of the fat man against the reduction in the great pain of the child.

Rights Theory

How does Rights Theory deal with this situation? Shoving the fat man is, of course, okay in Utilitarianism, but how does Rights Theory regard it? The possible implications of Rights Theory – although only if taken to its logical extreme – are that it is wrong to cause suffering (however trivial) to individual A regardless of the benefits (however great) to individual B. So, according to this point of view, we would not be allowed to shove the fat man even if, instead of a child, he was sitting upon a nuclear release button that would, if pressed for a determined period of time, cause the destruction of the world and in the process, utmost agony to individuals. Such an ethical theory is clearly absurd. Surely the trade-off here would be so advantageous that we must accept it.

I do not want to be accused of misrepresenting those who advocate the rights position for humans or nonhumans. They do not take the extreme position I have just depicted. Instead, they would invoke conflicting rights, such as the right to self-defence or a right to prevent aggression. These modifications to their pure theory, however, seem to be untidy and arbitrary. It is too easy to go on inventing various rights and giving to them some convenient priorities. Why should a right to prevent aggression have greater weight than a right not to be caused pain? Do *my* rights have more weight than *yours*? Why should a right to equality have priority over a right to liberty?

The trade-off problem that arises from conflicting rights is really central to all ethical theories. It seems to me to be so problematical that some sort of flexibility in ethical theory has to be accepted. Rigid principles, if they are extreme, can lead to absurd consequences: either to the Utilitarian absurdity of allowing torture if it proves to be very beneficial to others, or to the extreme Rights Theory absurdity of permitting agony in order to avoid inflicting even mild inconvenience on those who are the cause of that agony.

Two further problems

My own early publications on ethics concerned the appalling suffering that I saw human beings inflicting upon nonhuman animals in laboratories.[7] Although my conclusions apply to all painients, regardless of species, the example of the predicament of laboratory animals is a useful one. It illustrates, for example, two additional ethical problems: first, with *deliberately* causing pain that otherwise would not have occurred and, secondly, with the disparity in *certainty* or probability between causing pain now and justifying it in terms of benefits that may or may not occur sometime in the future. In a painful experiment, the pain is certain, but the benefits are always uncertain.

Let us briefly look at these two problems. The first can be put in the form of the question: if it is wrong to cause pain, is it more wrong to do so deliberately than inadvertently? Most ethicists, from whichever school, would agree that, prima facie, it is more wrong to cause pain deliberately. This immediately puts the experimenter into an even weaker position. He or she has to justify actions that involve the deliberate infliction of pain. As we know, of course, this attempted justification usually takes the form of some version of the trade-off argument. That is, the experimenter argues that causing pain to A is justified because of the benefit to B. This, incidentally, was the approach used by those defending Nazi scientists after the Second World War. It was claimed that the pain they had caused prisoners used in research was justified by the benefits achieved in terms of the consequent treatments for illnesses and injuries that their experiments uncovered. These defences failed in a court of law and many were convicted.

There are those who consider that there is a very considerable difference, morally speaking, between *deliberately inflicting* pain

and *not intervening* to stop or reduce pain that is occurring naturally. One cannot, practically speaking, spend one's life trying to
stop natural pain occurring everywhere, but one can seriously try
to avoid deliberately causing pain oneself. The sin of commission
seems far worse than the sin of omission. On the other hand, the
sufferers of pain do not care how their pain is being caused, they
only desire that it should be reduced. Both animal welfarists and
genuine medical researchers may be motivated by the same desire
to reduce the suffering of others. Yet the latter accept that they can
deliberately inflict pain on A in order (they hope) to reduce naturally occurring pain in B. Animal welfarists, on the other hand, and
certainly those who see themselves as animal rightists, tend to
reject this argument and deny that good ends justify such bad
means. The good intentions of a torturer do not reduce the pain of
his victim. It is ethically dubious, surely, to become more concerned with the motives of the pain causer than with the experiences
of the sufferer. It is the latter that is important morally. Indeed, we
can make this another rule:

*Rule 17: The experiences of the moral patient are always of
greater moral importance than the motives of the moral agent.*

So it is not motives that we are concerned with in making rational
moral judgements. It is the consequences of our actions that matter.
But surely there is a legitimate distinction to be made between
pains that are deliberately caused (and could, therefore, easily have
been avoided) and those that inevitably occur due to causes beyond
our control – or, indeed, beyond anybody's control? This is, however, a purely practical distinction. Of all the pains in the world
there are some that we can easily prevent. These are, surely, our
front line in the war we constantly wage to reduce the pains of
others. The degree of difficulty of reducing the pains of others
probably varies smoothly from relatively easy cases (e.g., don't
hunt animals for fun and don't hit innocent strangers) through more
challenging examples (e.g., don't eat meat and don't fail to help
old ladies) to far harder instances (e.g., don't let babies starve in
Africa and don't let sick rodents be denied veterinary treatment in

Kuala Lumpur) to, frankly, impossible situations (e.g., don't allow earthquakes to cause any suffering).

Somehow we believe that we are more culpable for our positive actions than for our omissions. It is as if we feel that sins of commission are worse than sins of omission because they entail more effort on our part. But this is attaching too much importance to the agent. We must remember that what matters morally are the consequences for the sufferer. One cannot, as Jonathan Glover aptly puts it, accept that acts and omissions with identical consequences can vary in moral value.[8]

The second special ethical problem facing the animal researcher commencing an experiment is that the hoped-for benefits of the research still lie in the future. Scientists are especially sensitive to the difficulties of prediction. Whereas in the case of the hypothetical fat man, it is almost certain that a strong shove will dislodge him, thus alleviating the child's pain, it is far less certain that a particular experiment will have a beneficial result. I believe this makes the case against painful research even stronger. It involves a trade-off between real pain and hypothetical benefit. Similar situations arise daily in our human to human interactions.

Quite separate from the question of the severity or degree of pain (i.e., some combination of its intensity and duration) is the probability or certainty of its occurrence. It is all very well to argue that we should cause mild pain to A in order to reduce the huge pain of B. But how certain are we that we will achieve this desired result? We are often going to be more certain of the causing of pain to A than of reducing the pain of B because the former is more under our control and nearer to us in time. In grey areas of this sort we need another rule of thumb.

Rule 18: The probability of reducing the pain of B should always be at least as great as the probability of causing pain to A.

I am not trying to say that I have eased the trade-off problem. It has plagued ethics for centuries and will continue to do so. Would it be justified to experiment painfully on one non-consenting human being in order to produce, with absolute certainty, a widely applicable cure for cancer? If so, how much pain in the experiment would be justified – severe agony lasting for weeks? If not, would a short twinge? (Of course, humans may be able to understand better what is happening to them than can nonhumans. Sometimes this will reduce their total suffering and sometimes it will have the opposite effect.)

The trade-off problem remains very awkward. A simple solution to the problem, either way, causes difficulties. So if one is to permit trade-offs at all, they had better be under very special conditions. For example, my theory would never permit causing pain to others in order to reduce the pain of maximum sufferers to absolute zero. If, in order to reduce the pain of the maximum sufferer A, it is necessary to cause pain to B, then this trade-off could only ever be justified to the point *where the pain of A is reduced to the same level as the pain of B.*

In formulating the above rules I am not trying to be doctrinaire. Rules have to remain flexible in ethics. They should be regarded merely as useful guidelines that will assist in making quick decisions. Each case, strictly speaking, needs the consequences of alternative courses of action to be calculated in terms of their algesic effects. In practice, we cannot always do this, so having rules of thumb becomes important. Where the rules do not fit then perhaps we should follow the drift of 'situation ethics' which suggests that we should do whatever is the most *loving* thing.[9]

Double standards

A concern for the individual is often a basis for laws protecting humans but not for those protecting nonhumans. The latter are almost invariably based upon Utilitarian principles where the suffering of an individual can be justified in the name of a greater total benefit to others. Hence the typical offence is to cause *unnecessary* suffering. In most laws protecting humans, however, each individual is protected absolutely. For example, it is considered wrong to experiment upon a human being without consent (except in certain entirely risk-free cases), even if that experiment may bring some advantage to others. This is despite the fact that with human rather than nonhuman subjects the likelihood of achieving useful results would certainly be higher. Why is there this speciesist double standard? Clearly, because of human self-interest.

Speciesism

I first published an attack upon what I called *speciesism* while I was working in Oxford in 1970. The term had several advantages, so it seemed to me, over other concepts in use. First, it drew the parallel with other forms of unfair discrimination such as ageism, racism and sexism. Secondly, it avoided the use of the word 'rights', which is traditionally disliked in Britain. Thirdly, it helped me to get across my own distinct ethical view. I attacked what I saw as an almost universal blind-spot in conventional morality – the then exclusion of nonhuman animals from serious ethical consideration. I published my thoughts in leaflets, books and letters to newspapers.[10] This attracted considerable opposition and ridicule, but also support from the writer, Brigid Brophy. Within a matter of months a small group of concerned reformers had formed in Oxford, including the philosophers Roslind and Stanley Godlovitch, John Harris and Peter Singer. The latter espoused and promoted the use of the concept of speciesism, giving it credibility and widespread currency. By 1985, 'speciesism' was in the Oxford English Dictionary, defined as 'discrimination against or exploitation of certain animal species by human beings, based on an assumption of mankind's superiority'.

My attack on speciesism was based upon my belief that nonhuman animals share with humans the capacity to suffer pain and distress. I drew attention to the scientific evidence that supported this view and reminded my readers (and later, television and radio audiences) that one of the moral implications of Darwinism is that animals and humans are in the same moral category. I argued that there is no morally relevant difference between most nonhuman and human animals. I collected evidence to show that some other species are highly intelligent, can make tools and use sign languages, while pointing out that these similarities are interesting rather than morally significant. *The morally crucial similarity remains our common capacity for suffering*. I argued that morality should be based upon this painience and that pain in a human has no greater moral significance than the same amount of pain in a nonhuman.

At the time, in the early 1970s, such ideas were sometimes considered revolutionary and deeply shocking. Today they are, I am glad to say, widely accepted. Also prevalent then was the widespread view that a difference in species was entirely unbridgeable and represented an absolute biological and moral divide. I produced evidence that many species, including primate species, could interbreed producing fertile hybrids and predicted that, in the future, the production of human/animal hybrids would expose the irrationality of conventional morality. This is now happening with the production, through genetic engineering, of transgenic animals containing human genes.

In conclusion, we acknowledge that the human species is but one of many species. We know that other animals often behave as we do when in pain and that their nervous systems and their brain biochemistries are similar to our own. Since Darwin we have known that nonhumans are related to us through evolution. It is inconsistent, therefore, to continue to put our own species on a moral pedestal entirely separate from all the others and to treat other animals not as relations but as things. Pain is the common enemy of all animal species. The conscious life of an individual does not endure for long but while it does we ought to try to reduce the suffering it contains.

Painism and the environment

Quite often the assumption is made that the revived concern for animal protection is a by-product of the environmental movement. It is certainly the case that, in the 1960s, environmentalism surfaced just before animal liberation burst upon the scene. However, it is also true to say that environmentalism does not have the same highly developed ethical underpinnings. Modern animal protection has, to an extent, been led by professional philosophers. Maybe, because it often goes against selfish human interests, animal protection actually needs this power of argument behind it. Environmentalism, in contrast, is largely driven by self-interest – I want to preserve beautiful rivers, clean air and biodiversity usually for my own ends.

I have divided environmentalism into seven types, most of which are anthropocentric, and I call these, respectively, thrifty environmentalism, aesthetic, scientific, historic, health conscious, compassionate and mystical environmentalism, according to their principal psychological motive. The thrifty environmentalist is concerned to save energy and resources, the aesthetic to preserve beauty, the scientific to protect what is of scientific interest, the historic to do likewise for things of historic value and the health-conscious is concerned about threats to human health caused by pollution, radiation and so on. Only the last two types of environmentalism, the compassionate and the mystical, escape the narrow confines of anthropocentrism and show a broader concern for the suffering of creatures for their own sakes, and for nature generally. Basically, there are four alternative ethical positions revealed by these approaches; a concern for all *natural features* (including rocks and rivers and other non-painients), a concern for the *whole environment*, including human-made features such as buildings, a concern for all *life* (including non-painient plant life) and a concern for all *painient* things (which is my own position). Environmentalists of other types need not fear painism, however, because all their concerns are subordinate to painism in the sense that damage or destruction of rocks, rivers, beautiful, historic, or scientifically valuable objects, are bound to cause suffering to the animals who inhabit these features or to humans such as themselves. They are thus all issues of concern to painists.[11]

In his classic 1989 paper J. Baird Callicott described a triangular relationship between animal liberation, the land ethic of Aldo Leopold, and conventional humanism.[12] I believe that all three are subordinate to painism and I cannot accept any form of environmentalist ethic that gives rights to non-painient things such as rocks and rivers. Such things have undoubted value, but this lies solely in the pain and pleasure that they give to painients. Ecosystems and species are also, per se, non-painient so their protection is not a moral end in itself.

The Animal ethicists

Three distinct ethical positions are represented by Peter Singer, Tom Regan and myself. All of us began by attacking the exploitation of nonhuman animals[13] and we have all gone on to apply our ethical views to the treatment of human beings also. All of us are deeply opposed to speciesism and so see no reason why our ethical concerns for humans and nonhumans should be significantly different. The details of our ethical theories, however, do differ. Peter Singer is a Utilitarian, Tom Regan is a Rights Theorist and I am a painist. I agree with Singer that pain is the crucial issue, but disagree with his Utilitarian aggregation of the pains and pleasures of several individuals. I disagree with Regan's view that it is the inherent value of an animal that matters. This is a bit too vague for me. I prefer pain (broadly defined) as the basic criterion of what is wrong. But I agree with Regan's emphasis on the importance of the painient individual. It is the suffering of each individual that matters.[14] (See Table below)

The Position of Painism compared with Utilitarianism and Rights Theory

Three ethical positions	Utilitarianism (Singer)	Painism (Ryder)	Rights Theory (Regan)
Basic criterion is pain	Yes	Yes	No
Some individual trade-offs allowed	Yes	Yes	Yes/No
Aggregation of the pains/pleasures of many	Yes	No	Yes/No
Against speciesism	Yes	Yes	Yes

Peter Singer's view is that there is no ethical justification for failing to extend the basic moral idea of equality of consideration to animals. If an animal feels pain then the pain matters as much as it does when a human feels the same degree of pain. 'Speciesism is logically parallel to racism and sexism.' The only justification for causing pain, says Singer, is if the aggregated benefits of all those affected by the action outweigh the pain.[25]

Tom Regan argues that animals have a biography as well as a biology – 'each has a life that fares better or worse for the one whose life it is, a life that includes a variety of biological, psychological and social needs and interests'. As with humans, each individual animal has 'inherent value'. The most fundamental right of each individual is 'to be treated with respect'.[16] If we consider the 'trade-off' situation it can be seen that Utilitarianism has no qualms about saying that I should cause pain to A in order to reduce the greater pain of B. Rights Theorists, however, would have to argue that the rights of B take precedence over the rights of A. Often, Rights Theory is presented as being more extreme than Utilitarianism yet all good Rights Theorists admit there has to be provision for sensible trade-offs under some circumstances – we must be allowed, for example, to cause trivial suffering to A in order to prevent the utmost agony of B. Tom Regan reveals the difficulty of the trade-off issue:

> I do not believe causing pain to the innocent (harming them) can *ever* be justified because of the benefits others derive; the right to be treated with respect is *never* to be violated or overridden; the rights of animals makes every form of their routine exploitation (vivisection, farming them for food, etc.) wrong from the get-go; and the only thing that can override one right is another right, so that if rights conflict, whatever the right thing to do is is (a) not to be determined by aggregating harms and benefits but (b) is to be determined by determining which, if any, right takes precedence.[17]

In the above statement, Regan begins by asserting that 'the right to be treated with respect is never to be violated' but, quite rightly, goes on to qualify this by saying that 'the only thing that can override one right is another right'. If rights conflict, one has to determine 'which, if any, right takes precedence'. How is this to be done? On what is this 'precedence' to be based? The answer is that it seems to be based upon intuition.

Regan also touches upon this problem in his classic *The Case for Animal Rights*, first published in 1983, by proposing two principles.[18] First, the *Miniride Principle* asserts that when faced with choosing between overriding the rights of the many or of the few 'then we ought to choose to override the rights of the few'. Secondly, the *Worse-Off Principle* provides an important exception to the miniride principle to the effect that 'when the harm faced by the few would make them worse-off than any of the many would be . . . then we ought to override the rights of the many'. Both principles, Regan says, are derivable from his *Respect Principle* that stipulates that we are to respect the inherent value of other individuals regardless of species (op. cit., p. 248). The order of precedence of rights is not always clearly set out by Rights Theorists and this is a pity because without some such hierarchy of rights it will often be impossible to decide on the morally correct way to act when rights come into conflict. Without such rules, Rights Theory has a hollow centre. When faced with conflicting rights, which right do we choose?

It is certainly true that rights have a hard shell-like quality and so, in discussing moral dilemmas in general, 'rights' are sometimes considered to 'trump' all other benefits. They are treated as absolute – the right to life, for example, is often taken to override all other considerations. This idea that rights provide protective barriers around individuals has often been invoked to avoid the worst consequences of Utilitarianism. For instance, the woman whose gang rape can be justified in Utilitarian terms if the aggregated pleasures of all the rapists outweigh her pains, can thus be protected by invoking *an absolute right not to be raped.*

In my opinion it seems highly desirable to erect a rights fence (specifically incorporating the right not to be subjected to pain) around human and nonhuman individuals alike, over which the rights of others can only take precedence if they reach a very high level. This conforms with Rule 14 (p. 30, above). *It is never justified to inflict any involuntary pain on A in order to reduce the pain of B unless the pain of B is of severe intensity.*

The theory of painism comes somewhere between Utilitarianism and Rights Theory. It shares with Utilitarianism its focus upon pain but rejects its aggregation principle. On the other hand it shares with Rights Theory its emphasis upon the importance of the individual but rejects any mysterious references to *telos* (purpose) or to intrinsic values.

Free will

The whole question of responsibility and culpability before the law depends upon the assumption that, in some sense, we can freely choose how we behave. We, as individuals, are held responsible. It is we, not our actions, that are in the dock. When someone is murdered, it is the murderer who is tried, not the murderous behaviour. Perhaps this is naive, yet it would be strange if the accused could join the jury and participate in a judgement on whether or not the murder was wrong. The assumption is always made in murder trials that the individual collection of bodily cells and tissues that is in the dock, in some intrinsic way represents the murderous behaviour. This assumption is made even years after the alleged crime when the cells in the body have changed and the individual may be quite different (except for his continuing memories) from the individual who once long ago acted murderously.

We certainly tend to *believe* that we can decide our own actions but there is some scientific evidence that this is merely an illusion. Benjamin Libet,[19] for example, has shown, in a number of crucially important experiments, that people begin to initiate an action fractionally before they are aware of making the decision. He asked students to record when they decided to initiate an act (e.g., the raising of a finger). On average, they reported that they first became aware of their intention to do so about 200 milli-seconds before they moved. Yet EEG recordings of electrical patterns in their brains showed increased activity around 500 milli-seconds before any movement. It seems, therefore, that the decision to act only emerged as a conscious wish about a third of a second after the process started. The movement of the finger may still have been 'willed' but it must have been willed pre-consciously. Nevertheless, experiments of this sort confirm what is, today, commonsense – that it is the state of our brains that determines behaviour and that our brains are physical systems in the same sense that a television or a lawn mower is a physical system. If a lawn mower goes out of control and kills someone, should we, therefore, put it in the dock and charge it with murder? I think we have to regard responsibility for our actions in the light of such considerations. Clearly, our behaviour is determined. We are not entirely to blame for our actions although we all tend to believe that we are.

Consciousness, said T. E. Huxley, is like the whistle on a steam train; although it attracts much attention it really makes little difference to the speed or direction of the train. Recent research suggests that (in cases of so-called 'blindsight') we can perceive without being conscious of seeing, and that our emotions emerge in the brain well *before* we are aware of them. Conscious or not, however, we are, it seems, entirely the slaves of our brains.

However, there are two major caveats that seem important. The first is that our ideas of what is right and wrong are among the many influences that act upon our brains. Ideas must have a physical basis in the brain. So moral ideas *will* affect our brains and our actions. The second point is a much more subtle and important one and is that, as physics advances, so it becomes apparent that the universe is not determined by rigid laws of nature, as Isaac Newton once envisaged, but by unpredictable events at the quantum level. Sub-atomic particles show free will rather as we ourselves do. I am not saying that they are conscious, but they act unpredictably. Our brains also produce effects that are unpredictable. There should be no shame in admitting that we are machines governed by the laws of physics since we know that the laws of physics are amazingly subtle. Apparent 'free will' is a part of physics and present in all physical systems. Reducing the mind to brain tissue may upset some people, but this is not a reduction to something dull and mechanical. It is, on the contrary, a 'reduction' to something marvellous and complex and unpredictable. The laws of physics are, themselves, more strange than any dream.

Some thoughts on pleasure and pain

As we are postulating that pain (and pleasure) are centrally important in ethics we will now spend a short time considering some of the psychological questions raised by these experiences. In my opinion, pains fall into three main types. These are painful *sensations*, painful *emotions* and painful *thoughts*. (I am using 'pain' to cover all negative experiences – all forms of suffering.) These can be further subdivided. As we have seen (p. 32) painful sensations can, at least, be divided into seven main types of pain that can be described as burning, stabbing, gnawing, pulling, aching, throbbing or stinging.[20] Painful emotions range from fear, disgust and grief to shame and guilt. (I include anxiety as an important and, sometimes enduring, type of fear. Anger in its raw state is analgesic rather than painful. It is guilt that causes the pain that is often associated with anger and its effects.) Painful emotions tend to have cognitive accretions such as our thoughts of the object of our fear, and the causes of our grief, disgust, shame and guilt. For example, I feel ashamed of my knobbly knees or guilty about my disloyalty to Bloggs. But *thoughts* per se can also be painful. The thought of death or disease or other ugliness is, in its purely 'emotionless' form, painful too.

The magnitude of pains (of all types) can be rated according to their level of intensity and also according to their duration. Pains can be measured, but only approximately, by their physiological effects such as alterations in the autonomic nervous system leading to changes in respiration, blood pressure and heart rate and levels of hormones such as catecholamines and cortisol. Tests of preference behaviour are another objective way to measure the effects of pains, although preferences provide no absolute scale. Once pain is experienced then it causes general arousal and a number of emotions – basically fear but also, as a defence, anger. Overall mood state (depression or mania) is affected by pain and, paradoxically, also affects the perception of pain. Even painful sensations are highly 'psychological' and involve higher cortical areas of the brain such as the frontal lobes. If these are out of action then pain can seem less important. Chronic pain almost invariably leads to depression which is, itself, a quintessentially painful condition that tends to amplify pain. Acute pain can lead to shock – faintness, sweating and breathlessness, itself an extremely painful condition. So pains can amplify themselves in vicious circles of this sort. Painful sensations cannot, however, be accurately measured by degrees of external physical injury. Patrick Wall has described how frequently 'physical' pain does not ensue immediately after severe physical damage. A man may lose a leg in battle and, at first, feel almost nothing. The brain itself produces its own painkilling chemicals (endorphins) and Wall and Melzack have shown that incoming pain signals can be blocked by descending signals from the brain.[21] In general, chronic pain is worse than acute pain. The latter is sometimes a useful warning that brings compensatory benefits to the individual. Chronic pain, on the other hand, often seems pointless.

Pains (suffering) can also be divided into *pains of deprivation* (e.g., hunger, loneliness, boredom and other failures to satisfy a need or drive state) and *pains of stimulation* (e.g., pains caused by extreme temperature, threat, noise, injury, insult etc.). One can also call these *indirect* and *direct* pains respectively. The indirect pains of deprivation have been central to the field of psychology. Post-Freudians have postulated the importance of oral needs (originally milk from the mother's breast) and the sexual drive. Frustration of these instinctive needs (collectively called the id) caused by external or internal (superego) factors flouts the pleasure principle and causes psychic pain. The Behaviourists, too, have postulated an array of needs and drives from hunger and thirst to parental and reproductive drives which, when unsatisfied lead to activity and stress. Animals seek to avoid states of dissatisfaction and are rewarded when their drives are reduced or satisfied. Other schools of psychology have listed other, more subtle, needs and drives (for cognitive consonance, security, meaning, adventure, sense of self-esteem, status, self-identity etc.). Overall, it is generally accepted that the satisfaction of drives and needs is one of the main sources of pleasure or reward for any animal.

Pain (suffering) is often defined as a emotion. I do not accept this. Pain *causes* emotions (anger and fear chiefly) and itself is an attribute of certain thoughts, sensations and emotions. Pain also demands attention and disrupts ongoing thought and behaviour. In itself it becomes a most powerful drive, motivating the sufferer to seek immediate pain-reduction. Is there, then, any other motivation than drive-reduction? Does a totally satiated animal remain inert? Anyone who keeps well-fed adult cats may well ask this question – they sleep contentedly hour after hour! Yet even satiated and neutered cats, particularly young ones, eventually appear to become bored and sally forth to find (often destructive) adventure. Is this action merely caused by increased 'boredom-drive'? Is drive-reduction (food, sex, status, etc.) the only type of pleasure or are there some pleasures that are *additional* to complete satiation?

Consider a stereotypical satiated person – the pampered potentate sitting upon his divan surrounded by wine, women and music. Is there anything more that he can possibly want? There is a semantic problem here. As soon as he manifests a search for some apparently additional pleasure it is possible to argue that there was also a corresponding unsatisfied drive. If, for example, the potentate insists upon starting a war, one can postulate that he had an unsatisfied war drive (aggression) or a drive for fame or glory. Despite this problem with the drive concept, to reject entirely the language of drives would be to throw an important psychological baby out with the bathwater. Nevertheless, I am inclined to believe that there are some pleasures which are not dependent upon our internal drives. I do not feel much of a drive for beauty but when I see it I find it pleasurable. Sometimes I do not feel much of a drive for music or massage, for sweet perfumes or jokes or for fascinating ideas or hearty exercise, but when I find them then I enjoy them. I know one can learn to seek these things because they have proved in the past to be rewarding. Such secondary drives cloud the picture. But I am still not convinced that the only pleasures are drive-reductions. Even when entirely drive-satiated I can still enjoy Beethoven. Like pains, I believe that pleasures, too, can be put into two main categories – the indirect pleasures of satiation and the direct pleasures of stimulation.

Are, then, pain and pleasure on the same dimension? Is negative pain pleasurable? Is negative pleasure painful? Is there a neutral state in which we are neither in a state of pain nor pleasure? None of these questions are easy to answer. Nor is the relation between pleasure and happiness. The latter is probably the most important question for ethics if one postulates one overall ethical aim – as in Utilitarianism, to increase the happiness of others. What is meant by happiness? The satiation of all drives? If so, what are they? Does happiness ensue automatically in the absence of all pains including the pains of stimulation? We know that unsatisfied expectations (perhaps because they are unrealistically high) are a potent and common cause of unhappiness.

Aristotle used the term *eudaimonia* to describe the condition at which we can aim. It has been translated variously as happiness, well-being or success. It includes pleasures but goes beyond them. It is a lasting condition of fulfilment or calmness rather than ecstasy or excitement. Contentment might be a good word for it. Somehow, however, the questions remain. We can agree that 'pleasure' is not the same as 'happiness'. Is happiness, then, the sum total of pleasures in the absence of any pains? Possibly. But are we happier when our hunger is satiated or in the process of satiating it? We don't ask our friends after dinner so often as we invite them to dine with us.

It would be wrong, of course, to omit a mention of Epicurus (341–270 BC) who believed that only pleasure is good in itself. However, pleasure, in Epicurus' theory, was approximately equivalent to the absence of pain. Furthermore, he distinguished between two types of pleasure – an underlying harmonious state of mind and more fleeting 'kinetic' (or sensual) pleasures. He preferred the former. Once the underlying state of harmony, *ataraxia*, had been achieved then there was no way to increase pleasure. Yet this peace of mind is particularly vulnerable, said Epicurus, to fear, especially the fear of the gods and the fear of death. Epicurus was, like Bentham later, convinced that both the dominant motivation in life as well as the object of virtue were the maximisation of pleasure and the minimisation of pain. Epicurus particularly recommended friendship, self-knowledge and the removal of unnecessary desires in order to achieve *ataraxia*. *Ataraxia* (peace of mind) is similar to Aristotle's *eudaimonia* (well-being). Both have been identified with happiness rather than with pleasure.

I do not really want to get sidetracked into an argument about the relationship between pain and unhappiness. We all know that pain is more specific than is unhappiness. Unhappiness tends to

be a more generalised mental state. Secondly, pains, thank goodness, tend to be more fleeting. They come and they go. Unhappiness, on the other hand, can endure for weeks or months or even
for years. Unhappiness is very similar to depression. It is more like
a mood than a simple emotion such as grief. Is there then no cor-
relation between pain and unhappiness? Certainly there is. The
more pain that is experienced the greater is the probability of unhappiness. But some people remain remarkably cheerful while they
are in pain. Almost certainly this is a defensive reaction at the
neurochemical or cognitive levels. Also, we know that frontal lobe
damage can produce a feeling of indifference towards pain. We
should note that there is a two-way relationship between pain and
mood. Depressed moods can sometimes be deepened or lightened
by external events when these are, respectively, painful or pleasurable. More severe depressions, however, appear to have a life of
their own, independent of changes in the environment. When
depressed, even quite neutral events can seem painful. The psychological picture is interesting but complex. Suffice it to say that
pain and unhappiness are highly correlated. From the ethical point
of view we are, I suppose, ultimately interested in unhappiness.
On the other hand pain, in all its many varieties, is easier to study.
Pains are less nebulous and more discrete. This is why I talk of
my own ethical position as *painism* rather than as *sufferingism* or
unhappinessism![22]

Various conclusions emerge from this discussion. Neither pain
nor pleasure are easy concepts. Both take multiple forms. Both are
fundamental to behaviour and both are central to ethics. Pain,
however, is not only more distinct and more motivating than pleasure; it is also slightly easier to understand. So painism appears to
be an easier ethic to use than hedonism. (I reject entirely J. S. Mill's
prudish assertion that some pleasures are morally superior to others
and agree with Bentham that the pleasures of pushpin are as good
as those of poetry.) In general there is less dispute about pain. We
can always recognise it and we always detest it. In a sense, too, it
is less imperatively my duty to give pleasure than it is to alleviate
pain. If someone else is not actually suffering then it seems more
acceptable to leave to them, and to chance, the provision of their
own pleasures.

Rule 19: I conclude that pain is more powerfully wrong than pleasure is right.

Altruism

Morality, generally speaking, constrains our basic sexual, aggressive and acquisitive impulses and those moral codes that have tended to produce behaviours with high social survival value have, obviously, tended to survive. Hence, no doubt, the survival of societies that value certain altruistic behaviours. Various innate impulses, such as compassion, harmonise with morality. It is unfashionable to regard compassion as an instinct, but altruism can be seen in other primates, in elephants and in dolphins who have sometimes been observed trying to help their stricken comrades. Charles Darwin himself noted that crows feed their blind and that chimpanzees form close supportive relationships. In its more narrow and intense manifestation, compassion is found as parental behaviour, which is one of the most powerfully driven of all animal instincts. Compassion can, of course, be directed, liberated and augmented by experience or, indeed, suppressed or poisoned by it. It can be smothered by the almost universal cult of machismo that teaches people that it is weak or, in some other sense, *wrong* to express compassion. Thus, this side of our natures is frequently concealed and stultified. Habituation, too, to the sight of blood and pain, can dull our compassion and related feelings of squeamishness.

I believe there are three innate reasons why we sometimes, quite naturally, want to help others. The first, as I have said, is *compassion*. The second is the deep *desire to earn the approval of others*. The third is our '*herd instinct*' when threatened by external dangers. These three all encourage altruism and are born into us because altruism has promoted the survival of our genes. Why? Because for hundreds and thousands of years our ancestors, physically weak bipedal apes, had to survive in a hostile environment surrounded by rivals and predators far stronger than themselves. As with other pack or troupe animals our safety has been in numbers. Isolated or entirely selfish individuals did not survive, while those impelled (through compassion, the desire for approval and the herd instinct) to help others triumphed and their genes flourished. Robert Wright, for example, argues: 'If caveman A and caveman B combine to hunt game that one man alone can't kill, both cavemen's families get a big meal; if there's no such cooperation, neither family does.'[23]

Our 'selfish' genes appear to have created brains that make us feel compassionate and cooperative because in that way they have spread copies of themselves. In particular we feel altruistic love for our children, their co-carers and for other kin. But compassion does not stop there. Evolutionary psychologists have argued that altruism must be based upon (a) an evolutionary advantage, and (b) a reciprocal advantage. It is worth examining these arguments.

Altruism and evolutionary psychology

First, does altruism have an evolutionary advantage? Does altruistic behaviour promote the survival of our genes? Clearly there are, as I have argued, occasions on which this must have been the case such as in the successful cooperation to catch prey or to defend the group. But there must also have been instances of altruism which led to the death of the altruistic individuals and to the obliteration of their genes. It is not, therefore, true that on *every* occasion the feelings of compassion, herd instinct or the desire for approval will work to the genes' advantage. Indeed, it is not even necessary, in principle, I believe, to insist that all behaviours have survival value. Overall, our behaviours have worked well from the point of view of natural selection but it seems quite possible that some of our repertoire of behaviours are 'by-products' or 'off-shoots' that have no survival value on their own. It may be that some acts of altruism, and their motives, are some of these, being offshoots or 'spill-overs' from the parental instincts which are known to be some of the most powerful motives in the animal kingdom.

Evolutionary psychologists have also argued that altruism is a form of disguised self-interest in which I help others in order to encourage them to help me at a later date. This is called *reciprocal altruism*. In 1966 George Williams suggested that compassion acts as an unconscious device for increasing evolutionary advantage by prompting others to repay our kindness.[24] Later, Robert Axelrod and Anatol Rapoport produced the theory that following the rule 'do unto others as they have done unto me' is a highly effective strategy. Specifically, Rapoport proposed to call this strategy 'tit for tat' according to which the most advantageous way for me to interact with others is to cooperate with them on first encounter and thereafter do whatever the other does: i.e., cooperate or withhold cooperation. Robert Wright, and others, have proposed that human societies are based upon this type of strategy: 'The daily life of every human society rests not just on reciprocity, but on a common foundation of feelings – sympathy, gratitude, affection, obligation, guilt, dislike and so on.'

These feelings, and others such as a 'sense of fairness' are, allegedly, born into us to motivate what has proved to be this very successful evolutionary strategy called reciprocal altruism. Such 'conditional niceness' is, says Wright, the only explanation of how we, and other animals, cooperate. Animals do not need to understand its logic – only to 'recognise individual neighbours and record their past deeds, whether consciously or unconsciously'.[25]

At least three problems bother me with the theory of reciprocal altruism. The first is, why do I feel compassion for koalas and caterpillars? Is there any realistic chance that they will repay my kindness? Will the koala give me gum leaves when I am starving or the caterpillar refrain from eating my cabbages? Clearly, my compassion in these cases – as in very many others – is not likely to be repaid at all. We could argue, again, that my compassion is a 'spillover' of feeling from the human to human situation or, even more specifically, from parent to child behaviour. But if so, is the theory of reciprocal altruism worth very much in explanatory terms? A second problem is quite similar. Why, in the human to human context, do I feel compassion not just for those who might be able to reciprocate but particularly for the very weak – for the unconscious, the crippled and the dying? These may have little or no power to reciprocate in the future. A third problem is that posed by the lower animals. Some ants, for example, can behave in highly altruistic ways, sacrificing themselves 'to the good of the colony'. It is highly unlikely that they can record the past behaviour of other individual ants in order to calculate their reciprocal advantages.

Their altruism is almost certainly genetically determined and very probably has survival value for their genes, but it cannot be called *reciprocal* altruism. One must conclude that any proposal that all altruism is disguised self-interest is unnecessairly cynical. It may be one source of altruism. But, surely, there are also others. Altruism as a purely cognitive ideal is one. Another, I would suggest, is the spill-over from parental or kinship feeling. Our altruism in such cases may come quite 'naturally' to us but it may not necessarily be to our advantage.

Here we should stop for a moment. What is it that we are discussing? We are trying to answer the question – why do we have this spontaneous desire to help others? Where does it come from? This is an interesting psychological question rather than a moral one. Are we using terms too loosely? Are we right to lump together altruism with cooperation, kindness and compassion? This is another area that may need further analysis. One must conclude, however, that the theory is less than complete. *The theory of reciprocal altruism, if true at all, can explain only a fraction of all the altruistic behaviour in the animal kingdom.* Similarly, kin altruism, or being kind to our kin, obviously has survival value for our genes, but sometimes I may not recognise my kin. Oedipus had this problem! He killed his father, not realising the relationship. On the other hand we can also feel spontaneous love for adopted but unrelated children and, indeed, for children in general. Once again, there seems to be evidence of a spill-over of compassion, way beyond the bounds of kinship.

There is now a great deal of evidence that those who are cruel to animals are often also outstandingly cruel to humans. Conversely, those who show a high level of empathy with humans also show a high level of empathy with nonhuman animals.

Killing

If pain is the only evil then what is wrong with painless killing? Dying naturally is often painful, so why not quietly and quickly kill people when they are fit, happy and least expecting to be killed? On the face of it, this could even look like being a moral duty. There are, however, three sorts of arguments against it. First, it is argued that by killing someone, one prevents that individual from experiencing all the remaining pleasures in his life. But if death results in total and permanent lack of awareness then surely the deceased cannot regret the loss of his future pleasures? Besides, one is also protecting the deceased from all the pains he would have experienced in his future. Secondly, it can be argued that people ought to have autonomy, or the capacity to choose. If someone wants to go on living it is wrong to kill them even if there are good grounds for believing it is not in that person's best interests to do so. But it remains unclear as to why autonomy has this moral importance. Perhaps autonomy's importance lies in the fact that being aware that one's autonomy is being thwarted makes one unhappy. But if one is dead one would not, presumably, be aware of this. Thirdly, by killing someone one may cause grief to that person's friends and relations. Even if he has none, anyone who hears about the killing may subsequently feel a sense of shock, live in fear of a similar fate, or experience some other painful feelings. The case of Dr Harold Shipman, who is believed to have killed scores of his reasonably healthy patients, comes to mind. After all the publicity of his trial many people felt less confident about putting their trust in doctors. They suffered feelings of insecurity. So this argument seems to be a good one. We can conclude that it is wrong to kill people humanely but without consent, at least because of the grief, insecurity and fear it may create in others.

Finally, there are considerations of *identity*. By destroying an individual we are destroying something subjectively unique. This applies to the killing of nonhumans, too. We are still left with the problem that of all the billions of complex brains now in existence I am aware of being in only one of them. Why is this? Why can I recall never having been alive previously? What is it that makes my brain 'mine'? If a different sperm of my father or a different ovum of my mother had once united would I now not be conscious of me at all? If my brain was progressively replaced by portions of others' brains would I remain me? As I have already argued, one can more or less accept that consciousness itself emerges from brain tissue rather as a television picture emerges from silicon and wires, but why this feeling of unique me-ness? If we kill an individual not only awareness but also that 'me-ness', so I believe, are ended forever. Although I am far from clear that this supports, per se, a right to life, yet the breathtaking scale and mystery of the question must surely give us pause. (Only when we can link our brains directly, for example, by cable, will such questions as 'identity' become severely blurred. If several individuals were to be linked in such a way that their painience became shared then they would have to be considered as an individual in moral terms.)

Conventional morality has a high regard for the sanctity of human life. But if killing by private individuals is so wrong then why is killing by the state deemed to be right? Surely, any president, governor or judge who has the power to stop a state execution and does not do so is guilty of murder? We should question whether such people should be tolerated in positions of power. Individual murders are usually driven by passion. State murders, in that they are cold-blooded, seem far worse.

The moral circle

The history of ethics can be seen as an ever-expanding circle of compassion. Starting, perhaps, as inclusive only of family and then tribal members it has widened to include others of the same nation, language or religion. For those outside these boundaries there was lesser moral status or, sometimes, no standing at all. Gradually, as the world has expanded and as humans have seen that foreigners and those of other races share with them certain common features, so prejudices have been eroded. Women and children have only recently gained equal moral status with men and, in some parts of the world, this is yet to be achieved. The final barrier is the difference in species of which Darwinism and modern genetic engineering make a nonsense. It is no longer tenable or rational to consider that there is a huge and morally significant gulf between human beings and the other animals. Such speciesism is as out of date and as unintelligent as racism or sexism. We are all a part of the animal kingdom and as subjects in that kingdom we all deserve equal respect. The moral circle should include all individuals (however small in size) capable of suffering pain or distress. It is our common painience that draws us together. Together we fight the common enemy that is pain.

Measuring pain

I have said that the moral importance of an issue is measured not by the quantity of individuals affected but by the degree of pain experienced by the maximum sufferers. Traditionally, we have tended to react with greater horror to reports of the massacres of many than to individual murders. When a plane crash kills 300 people we are more moved than when an individual pilot of a small private plane dies. Yet, in painist terms, this is irrational. What really matters in each case is the amount of suffering that was experienced by any one painient involved. In a car crash it may matter far more that someone was painfully injured than that someone was painlessly killed. Careless treatment in hospitals every day causes far more pain to individuals than does the armed robbery that attracts so much moral opprobrium on the front pages of newspapers. Each day individual children and animals are caused unnecessary agony by cruel, callous or unthinking people – these unreported events are of far greater moral significance than the public obsession with the number of hostages taken, the number of people killed in an earthquake or the number of passengers involved in a train accident. It is the quantity of pain per painient that is relevant, not the quantity of individuals affected. To torture a hundred political prisoners is no worse than torturing one. Each painient individual matters.

If this is the case then we need to develop more of an interest in measuring pain. This is already done, for example, under the administration of the Animals (Scientific Procedures) Act of 1986 where the expected pain of experimental animals is classified as either substantial, moderate or mild. Evaluations of pain are also done by the courts in assessing damages. Non-humans and human infants may, under some circumstances, suffer less because they do not anticipate impending death or disaster. At other times, however, their lack of a full understanding of what is happening will increase their suffering through increased fear. The 'F word' (fear) and the 'B word' (boredom) are particularly applicable to the sufferings of all captives, whether human or nonhuman. Some individuals are temperamentally more fearful than others. Sensitivity to all forms of pain, not only to fear and boredom, varies between individuals and between species. Even quite simple creatures such as insects learn to avoid noxious stimuli and behave generally as if they experience pain. Their experiences may be more simple than ours, but are they less intense? Perhaps a caterpillar's primitive pain when squashed is greater than our more sophisticated sufferings.

Behaviour itself is one way to measure pain but it is not very reliable. One could, for example, measure in decibels the intensity of the screams of injured individuals, but this is not likely to be accurately correlated with the intensity of pain experienced. Each species reacts differently to pain – injured prey species, for example, sometimes become quiet and still so as not to draw the attention of predators. More effective as a measure of pain are physiological indices such as autonomic responses (heart rate, respiration and galvanic skin response), or the level of hormones such as adrenaline, noradrenaline or cortisol, or of those brain transmitters associated with pain and its natural suppression by endogenous opiates. All these are possible measures and are enabling more rational decisions to be made, for example, in the care of animals. Where an individual is able to do so, he or she will naturally do all they can to avoid or reduce pain. By using such avoidance preferences animals can indicate to us what it is they find painful and what conditions are more painful than others. They can also be trained to 'do work' (e.g., pressing a lever or lifting a heavy door) to avoid unpleasant situations. By using such techniques – and self medication with analgesics is another – animals can rate their painful experiences for us. Pain remains a highly subjective experience for all of us and is dependent to a substantial degree upon psychological circumstances. Hypnosis, for example, can reduce or remove pain completely or, indeed, increase it, and in some hysterical conditions pain is similarly modulated. Removal of parts of the frontal lobes of the brain can produce an indifference to pain: the pain is still experienced but no longer seems to matter. *From the moral point of view, however, what is important remains the degree and the duration of pain **as it is experienced**.*

Conscience

I believe that the details of our moral sense, or conscience, are learned. But underlying whatever we learn to consider 'good' or 'bad' is the great inherent feeling of compassion that is in all of us, however hardened. Also present is our inherent and untaught feeling of justice that grows in us from childhood. Besides these we have the powerful and natural feeling of squeamishness at the sight of blood or injury. These three 'gut reactions' to the sufferings of others are our unselfish instincts and they need to be revered and built upon. We also have many other strong feelings that try constantly to drive us the other way, away from morality. These include our anger, rivalry, greed, fear, ambition and our desires to despise and dominate. These are selfish instincts. Morality itself is not an instinct. It is the product of reason built upon the foundations of those of our instincts that are unselfish. Morality can be based first upon our innate dislike of pain and then upon our natural sympathy for the suffering of others. These two premises do not need to be learned, but they can be unlearned.

Rule 20: Ethics is about unselfishness.

Conclusions

We can conclude as follows:

(1) Pain, broadly defined to include all forms of suffering, is the only evil. All other moral objectives are means to reducing pain.

(2) Around each painient individual is the boundary of consciousness. So it makes no sense to try to aggregate the pains of several individuals. (This is where painism parts company from Utilitarianism.)

(3) Each individual painient, of whatever race or species, is of moral importance.

(4) Of primary concern are those who suffer most – the maximum sufferers. Moral significance is not measured by the quantity of individuals affected by an action but by the degree of pain suffered by the maximum sufferers.

Some Applications

In this chapter I will try, as best I can, to apply the principles of painism to some everyday moral problems. I will include those issues, such as sex and genetic engineering, the moral importance of which I believe is customarily exaggerated, as well as topics that have been almost entirely overlooked by ethicists. In some instances I fail to discover the relevance of painism to the issues but conclude that all of them are morally significant. Nearly all aspects of our life have moral implications.

Abortion

We have already concluded that painlessly killing someone, without their consent, is wrong, not least because it creates pain and fear in others (*see* p. 61). In abortion it is a foetus that is killed.

When the parents want this to happen and where nobody else feels hurt at the prospect, can this be wrong? There are the usual arguments about the cutting off of the foetus' future pleasures, but against this one can argue that future pains are also being truncated. Nobody can predict exactly what sort of life lies ahead for the individual foetus. Where it is seriously handicapped then the prediction of future suffering for the individual and for its carers can be made with greater certainty and, in these circumstances, the decision to abort may prove morally easier. The same applies where the mother's life or health are, according to best expert opinion, put at serious risk unless an abortion is performed.

There are, however, four problems still to address. The first is a factual one. To what extent does abortion cause pain for the foetus? It is absurd to argue that painience suddenly appears at birth and does not exist in the womb. Abortion techniques are sometimes horrifically crude and almost certainly cause intense pain for the foetus.

Rule 21: All procedures which cause pain for the foetus are wrong prima facie. The foetus must be treated as a painient individual with all the moral protection that this entails.

At what juncture then does a foetus become painient? At two weeks of age, two months, six months? It is, of course, hardly necessary to answer this question if the abortion procedure itself is painless. If a foetus is painlessly anaesthetised before killing, then it is not necessary to find an answer to this difficult question.

The second point concerns the attaching of different rights at different stages of development. This is, surely, bound to be arbitrary. At one extreme, there have been moral codes which attach sacredness not only to mature life but even to ova and to semen. At the other, there are cultures in which the killing of unwanted neonates is regarded as acceptable. Here, again, the criterion must be painience and where there is uncertainty as to whether or not something is painient then, in my opinion, *the benefit of the doubt should always go to the potential sufferer.* If we accept that a foetus of, say, three months, is painient then does it have a lesser moral status than that of an adult? Surely it does not. One problem which follows from this is that, once this is accepted, whatever we judge to be morally right in our treatment of, say, three-month-old foetuses may also be right in our treatment of adults. If the capacity to indicate consent is taken into account, then we must say that a foetus is morally in the same position as an adult who cannot signify consent.

Thirdly, it is sometimes claimed that a foetus is not a separate individual but is merely a part of the mother and so has no separate rights. However, if our basic concern is painience then the correct question is this – *is the foetus, whether entirely separate or not, separately painient*? I believe that it can be.

Ultimately, abortion is an example of conflicting rights, chiefly, but not entirely, between foetal and maternal rights. The foetus, one can say, has a right not to suffer pain. If the mother's health or well-being is seriously threatened by the foetus then it is also a case of her right to not suffer pain due to ill health. Both, in addition, have a right to life due to the fact that both are individuals (*see* pp. 29ff. and 61) and in this respect I cannot see that their rights differ.

Rule 22: The rights of a foetus are the same as those of an adult of the same level of painience who cannot give consent.

Sometimes the consequences of unwanted births can include painful psychological effects for both mother and child. But in a culture where births out of wedlock have become socially accepted such considerations weigh less heavily. The pleasure that a baby may give to adoptive parents and others must also be borne in mind. So also should be the pains of all others including relatives, the doctors and nurses who have to perform the operation and even anti-abortion campaigners. In each case, our primary concern is for whoever suffers the most.

Clearly, much depends upon the circumstances in each case. Where there are no serious health risks involved either for the child or mother then we are dealing with a trade-off between the rights and interests of the foetus and those of others, who may include the father. However, if any individuals' distress at the prospect of abortion in a particular case is greater than any others' then that is the overriding right. I do not see that a father per se, nor a doctor, have, ex officio, any greater right. It must surely boil down to this – *who is suffering most*? Who is the maximum sufferer in each case? If it is going to be the foetus then the foetus must live. If it is the mother who, unless she has an abortion will suffer the most, then the abortion should proceed. If it is a friend who is distraught at the prospect, then, if they are suffering most, it is the reduction of *that* person's pain which becomes of primary importance. The effects of abortion can be very long lasting. I have met women grieving and suffering many years later over abortions to which they willingly agreed at the time.

One can only conclude that abortions are best avoided. But where the pain of the maximum sufferer dictates that this is the only course of action that will reduce their severe pain, then early abortions should be proceeded with, provided that the foetus itself suffers no pain in the process.

Siamese twins

Like a foetus and mother, Siamese twins are two conjoined individuals. Should such twins be separated? Is it possible for them to live happy lives while joined? Who can say with certainty? Once again, the problem is one of accurate prediction. If both have a good chance of survival if separated then, if they wish to be separated they should be. But usually such twins are infants who are unable to give consent. Is it wrong to separate them so that one will die but so that the other will have a good chance to live? Should the probable quality of life of the survivor be taken into account? These are all very difficult questions.

In a recent case before the British courts a judge ordered separation because, so he was advised, the consequences would be that one twin would die but the other would probably survive to live a handicapped but prolonged and intellectually normal life. However, he was also advised that if separation did not occur then both twins would sicken and die within about six months. So the choice was, in the opinion of some, between separation and killing one twin or no separation and allowing both to die.

Can painism help with such a difficult decision? If the predictions are accurate the alternatives appear to be between six months of suffering (for both) or a handicapped lifetime (for one). Yet many handicapped people live happy lives. According to painism, humane killing is not such a bad thing provided it does not upset others. In this case, the parents were extremely upset and opposed the separation on religious grounds. They opposed the relatively controlled and painless death of one twin in favour of a natural but probably distressing death for both.

Commonsense seems to suggest that separation would be right. The feelings of others are important but parents should have no special standing. Painism seems unable to help in such cases, chiefly because of the difficulty in predicting maximum states of suffering which will be the consequences of any decision.

This is an instance where the facts are so uncertain that painism cannot reasonably be applied.

Euthanasia

In the year 2000 the use of brain-dead people as organ donors spotlighted the almost incredibly stupid practice of some surgeons of removing organs from such people without the use of anaesthesia. The exact mechanisms of pain as an experience are still unknown. To assume that pain is only experienced in an intact and active brain is rash indeed. An apparently brain-dead person may still have areas of brain activity and these may be activated under conditions of extreme stimulation such as in unanaesthetised surgery.

Rule 23: As a general rule we should adopt the precautionary principle that, wherever painience is uncertain in a living animal it should be assumed to exist.

The general issue of human euthanasia has been much discussed by ethicists. With nonhumans it has long been argued in the West that their euthanasia is justified when their quality of life through disease, injury or infirmity has become, in the long term, irremedially painful or distressing. In some human cases – severe dementia, severe head injury, and wherever unconsciousness is expertly deemed to be irreversible, the moral case is similar. The individual herself is never going to be able to comprehend her situation or to give informed consent to euthanasia. There is surely a strong argument that, provided all those associated with the individual (doctors, nurses, relatives and friends) are not going to suffer greater distress if euthanasia occurs than the distress they are *already* suffering, then euthanasia should proceed. How, then, about human cases where consent has been given or specifically refused? Where euthanasia has been requested by the patient, and where all ways of treating depression have been tried, then surely this request should be acted upon, unless it would cause extreme distress to others. Where it has been expressly refused, that request, too, should be honoured. Where is the ethical difficulty? It seems largely to be bound up with archaic views on the 'sanctity' of human life. Such views are fine in that they encourage a respect for individuals, but such a respect is not going to be eroded, surely, by respecting the wishes of an individual to die. Wherever death is perceived to be the greater good or lesser evil for the patient (except where there is evidence of specific opposition to euthanasia by that individual patient) then it should be allowed to proceed.

Too often, the option of passive euthanasia is followed. That is to say, doctors opt not to treat a condition (e.g., they withhold resuscitation or they withhold fluids or food). In certain cases this can cause suffering and so should be avoided. *If withholding anything causes pain or distress then it ought not to be done.* It is far better to keep a patient well fed, comfortable and treated with medication that reduces pain and causes euphoria. There is no moral value, per se, in allowing a patient 'to die naturally'.

Rule 24: There is a duty upon those caring for the dying not only to administer enough analgesics to remove all pain but also to administer all appropriate psychoactive drugs so as to enhance the patient's sense of well-being until they die. Doctors have a duty not only to alleviate pain but to induce euphoria.

It has always seemed to me that ending one's life happily is more important than being happy earlier on. All's well that ends well. The contrary argument that 'it does not matter what this patient suffers as she is dying anyway' is, in my view, entirely irrational and deeply immoral.

Every effort should be made to create euphoria and to end life entirely peacefully. Euthanasia is a merciful scientific skill that needs to be actively funded, developed and valued by society. Medicine cannot always cure. Greater emphasis, therefore, should be placed upon helping people to die well. This means encouraging progress in the skills of anaesthesia, analgesia, causing euphoria and euthanasia. Care for the elderly, disabled and dying is one of the greatest goods in a civilised society. Their happiness is of particular importance. Any discrimination against the old because they are old (just as any discrimination against the young because they are young) seems irrational and wrong.

Doctors have been much attacked recently in the British media. Unlike most of us they are constantly faced with crucial moral decisions and so, like politicians, form an easy prey for the predatory press. In general, we are seeing far more internal discussion of ethics within the medical profession, a reduction in medical authoritarianism and a tendency to move towards the concept and application of informed patient consent.

Sex

Sexual behaviour continues to be a subject of great interest to the tabloid media who often affect concern about its ethical implications. This affected moral concern is chiefly a device whereby newspapers can increase their sales while protecting themselves against the charge that they are being prurient. Yet, despite the tabloids' apparent obsession with sexual morality, professional ethicists have devoted relatively little time to discussing the issue. Why is this? One can only assume it is because many serious philosophers consider that the moral implications of sexuality have, over the centuries, been considerably exaggerated. All cultures contain rules about sexual behaviour and several of the major religions – Christianity, Judaism and Islam among them – have placed particular emphasis upon this area of human behaviour. Sexual morality may have emerged as an issue partly due to the need to regulate the production and care of children, the protection of dependent mothers and the transference of property rights that, in many cultures, are associated with marriage. However, there may be other even more fundamental reasons. In as much as moral rules often cluster around human drives, containing and channelling them, they do so in particular where basic drives are in conflict. Sexual behaviour is one such crunch point. The sexual drive often comes into conflict with motives such as jealousy, possessiveness, the fear of infection, the need for security and the parental drive. In men and women these motives can differ slightly. Women (for good biological reasons) are programmed more to need security and to express parental feelings. For biological reasons, too, men are programmed to be promiscuous to a greater extent than are women. The long gestation period of the human species and the even longer period during which children depend upon their parents has favoured those with genes for caring, protecting and for maintaining long-term relationships. In conflict with these tendencies, some of those with promiscuous traits have also tended to disperse their genes effectively. So the desire to be promiscuous and the desire for a secure and lasting relationship are both born into us and are in conflict. It is hardly surprising, then, that at such a crossroads of human feelings, regulations should have been imposed. But today, with contraception, individual affluence and the treatment of many infections being readily available to both sexes, the situation has changed. In Western cultures, the taboos on birth outside wedlock, homosexuality, multiple partners, masturbation and other forms of sexual behaviour and its consequences, have been weakened. Where, then, do we stand on this issue at the start of the twenty-first century? Applying the principles of painism consistently we have to ask – is sex causing pain and if so to whom is it causing the greatest pain?

Rule 25: No sexual relationship is of itself wrong unless it causes pain.

Here is the greatest paradox of sex. The sexual act itself, and orgasm, far from being painful, are often experienced as the epitome of pleasure. So why should sex be wrong? If it causes ecstasy why should sex not become a moral duty rather than a form of behaviour surrounded by inhibitions and guilt? The answer is that besides causing ecstasy sex can and does also cause a wide variety of pains. Ironically, some of these pains are caused by the very same moral rules that may have been introduced initially to reduce them. Puritanical attitudes towards sex have caused massive human suffering over the centuries through the inculcation of shame and guilt. Cynical media, hiding behind the pretext of freedom of speech, today continue this cruelty. Working as a clinical psychologist in the 1960s I saw many people driven to despair and suicidal depression by feelings of guilt over their sexual desires and behaviour, and by the fear of exposure. Only twenty years later such cases had become far rarer, to be replaced occasionally by those who despaired for quite the opposite reasons – because they felt they were sexually under-active or insufficiently orgasmic.

There is now some scientific evidence that the psychological ingredients of sexual and loving relationships in both men and women can be divided into several separate but interrelated components such as physical attraction, affection, admiration and attachment. Love is probably a fluctuating amalgam of all these feelings at intense levels. Friendship (also a part of a stable, loving relationship) may contain some or all of these feelings, along with shared interests and enthusiasms. Any of these feelings when frustrated, unrequited or rejected, can cause pain. For this reason, love is a minefield. One of the causes of greatest pain is sexual infidelity, and so our concern should be with jilted partners generally. Can we lay down moral rules for infidelity? Is it always, regardless of circumstances, wrong? Surely not. Those prostitutes, mistresses, toy boys, gigolos and good lovers who conscientiously give sexual pleasure to others should be applauded. Prima facie they are doing good. Sometimes an affair can bring great pleasure and an enhanced sense of self-esteem to those involved, and to such an extent that other relationships (including those with long-term or marriage partners) are improved, at least while the affair remains secret. Knowledge of a partner's infidelity is almost invariably painful and so is the lack of trust engendered by telling lies about it. People frequently lose sexual interest in each other over time but may still wish to continue to live together for some of the other reasons mentioned – affection, admiration, attachment, shared memories and interests (the most powerful of which is usually an interest in the couple's children).

In nineteenth-century Europe, middle-class marriages were held together by powerful social sanctions. By the end of the twentieth century these had been relaxed and many couples today eventually separate, the partners adopting lifestyles of solitude, serial sexuality or enhanced friendships. As average standards of living rise, job opportunities for both sexes expand and family sizes reduce, so the average pain associated with the changing of partners is probably lessened (*see* the section on divorce law, below). Loss, the quintessential cause of reactive depression, is bound to occur, through death or separation, to every couple, sooner or later. The question is, how can we arrange our lives so that such deep pains due to the loss of a partner can be minimised? One way is to reduce the expectation that relationships last forever. Another is to encourage self-dependence. A third is to promote increased communal and extended family lifestyles. The widespread view in British society, for example, that children should leave home, could be discouraged. The idea that children must leave the family on maturity now appears to be anachronistic. It was, I believe, a nineteenth-century by-product of the process of Empire. Children (particularly boys) were required to leave home in order to build the nation's interests abroad through military and other forms of service and trade in the colonies. Before that time sons and daughters far more often stayed at home, helping domestically and with the family business. When married they may have moved, but to a nearby house from where they remained very often in working and supportive contact with other relations including parents. This sense of extended family succeeded in reducing the pains of loss and fragmentation that often confuse and cause suffering in society today.

Strangely, there are, in an age of assumed sexual liberality, still some areas of marked, if not increased, sexual suppression that cause considerable pain. I refer in particular to the widespread suppression of childhood and adolescent sexual drives. This suppression is caused largely by adult ignorance, envy and guilt. Although it upsets some adults to know this, children feel a strong interest in sex long before the intensification of their sexual feelings at puberty. Whereas in the past childhood sexuality was taken for granted, today it is often treated as scandalous. For centuries and throughout much of Europe, it was acceptable for young men to declare their love for girls aged 14 or 12 or even younger, and to marry them. However, girls today mature both physically and psychologically far earlier than they used to do. The average age of puberty (menarche) dropped from about 17 years of age in 1870 to around the age of 12 a century later. This means that adolescents today may, on occasions, be far *more* frustrated sexually than in the past. Yet, the disapproval and punishment of young teenage sexual behaviour has actually increased, especially if it involves a partner of either sex who is considerably younger or older, and today it has reached puritanical proportions. Is this just, or is it a form of ageism? Adults have been hounded mercilessly by the press. This must have caused intense suffering. Such attitudes, and the media persecution involved, seem unnecessarily cruel and deeply immoral. Very often the persecution appears far more wicked than the alleged offence.

Rule 26: Disapproval of sexual behaviour often causes pain and is, therefore, usually morally wrong. It should be made a criminal offence to persecute law-abiding individuals by publicising, without consent, their harmless sexual practices.

The liberalisation of sex in recent decades has sometimes led to a welcome reduction in painful sexual guilt. Yet it has also meant a loss of the intense pleasure associated with secret lust and passion. The only defence of puritanism is that it can have this aphrodisiac effect.

Prostitution gives much pleasure to clients but can also cause pain to the prostitute, her client or others. Girls forced into prostitution deserve the full and vigorous protection of the police. Consenting prostitution, however, should be legalised and properly controlled and protected. In this way its benefits would be maximised and its pains minimised. In general, because it is such a powerful source of pleasure, the sex industry should be more respected than it is. Prostitutes often deserve praise for the services they provide.

Certain forms of sexual practice, such as paedophilia, bestiality and incest, however, still incite intense public disapproval. Why is this? Of course, if these practices cause pain or distress, then they ought to be condemned. Yet there seems to be a lack of scientific evidence as to the extent of suffering caused. Young people, for instance, are often more robust than assumed. Where suffering occurs, as sometimes it undoubtedly does, there is a lack of rational debate about its causes. Is sexual experience in the young essentially painful? If so, is it more painful in young people than in adults? Is any such suffering caused not by the experience itself but by the aura of impassioned social disapproval surrounding it? What are the causes of the passionate feelings of outrage that are aroused? Is the violent disapproval displayed a product of rational concern? As a psychologist I have had to deal with such situations and have found that people quite often admit a degree of sexual interest in socially disapproved of practices, and that some of these become violent in their opposition to such behaviour in others. Sexually frustrated people can turn their envy of others' sexuality into puritanical disapproval. Controls are clearly needed but should be based upon more than emotion.

There are probably other motives, too, for the violent disapproval of paedophilia, such as feelings of inadequacy as parents. While a woman led a demonstration against an alleged paedophile in August 2000, her neglected three-year-old child was found wandering the streets of Portsmouth naked and in tears.[1] Sexual behaviour, whether it involves the very young or not is, of course, wrong if it causes unwanted pain or distress. Extreme taboos on certain forms of essentially unpainful sexuality, however, may increase the chances that their expression will be made furtive, violent and damaging for the victims. If forms of sexual behaviour are regarded as so shocking that the perpetrator is, literally, made afraid for his or her life, then, in extreme cases, murder of the victim can be motivated merely by a state of panic and as an attempt at concealment. Social disapproval thus creates the very evil it opposes. The genuinely violent or sadistic offender needs to be rigorously controlled and treated. But society will make matters worse if it turns more 'ordinary' sexual behaviour into violence or if the disapproval of it is itself traumatic for the victim. In Britain, over 90 per cent of murders of children are carried out by members of the child's family or close circle. Only approximately 7 per cent are done by strangers and some of these are not paedophiles. This is an area where high levels of emotion and the lack of scientific evidence cloud the issue. More research is needed before the ethics can be consolidated. But to destroy a man's family by sending him to prison *twenty years after* he had intercourse with a girl aged 14, as has recently happened, is morally outrageous, and to imprison a woman just because she has sex with a 14-year-old boy, seems to me to be monstrously immoral and an act of ridiculous injustice and cruelty. Such punishment (what effect does this imprisonment have on the woman's children?) is surely wicked and should be ended.[2] A boy of 14 is usually more than ready for sexual intercourse and perfectly able to consent to what is almost certainly for him a highly educative and pleasurable experience.

The persecution of President Clinton for some perfectly harmless sexual behaviour in the late 1990s was an example of cruelty made all the more revolting by the cynical, political and hypocritical underlying motives of his persecutors and the media. Yet those who were responsible for this cruelty escaped almost without censure. If the law was in line with morality, and if punishment was made proportional to the pain caused deliberately to others, then the President's tormentors should have been punished very severely indeed – at least as severely as those convicted, for example, of murder after provocation. The Clinton episode was the deliberate and cold-blooded public torture of a public figure. The continuing persecution of Clinton long after the event was one of the most disgusting manifestations of evil to be seen. Indeed, it seems to me disturbing evidence of the moral corruption that exists in American society – a society that widely promotes and accepts capital punishment, the private possession of firearms, gross social cruelties and crass materialism, often justifying these evils behind a mask of pseudo-Christian morality.

It is, however, important for the public to know of the *financial* interests of public figures. These should be out in the open. But if people wish their sex lives to remain private then they should be allowed to remain so. There should be far greater freedom of *public* information (e.g., about the business of governments and quangos and corporations and their financial interests) and far less invasion of the *privacy of individuals*. Governments have, quite wrongly, believed that they cannot legislate to protect individuals from media attention. The so-called 'freedom of the press' has become a sacred cow. It should be slaughtered. Governments can and should legislate to protect the individual. Freedom of speech is a great ideal but where it causes more individual pain than it reduces, it has lost its purpose and is wrong. Many British newspapers have become sewers from which flow the deceit, hypocrisy and moral filth of modern life. They lie, distort and accuse. They rarely, if ever, praise or applaud. They show scant respect for truth or justice. They cause great pain to their victims. Although they sometimes perform a genuinely useful role in revealing abuses of power, in their present form they have become morally unacceptable. They should be restrained.

What I have said above in no way condones paedophilia. If paedophilia causes pain then it must be condemned. However, it is far more likely to cause pain if society and the media react to it with hysteria, ignorance and sensationalism. Witch-hunts cause injustice and great suffering. They make a dubious situation far worse.

The bland society

In the most affluent parts of our planet we live in an increasingly bland society. Life is stressful – but bland. The struggle for existence has been replaced by the search for happiness. Yet we seem to feel less. Our emotions are deadened and our sensitivities blunted. Some of the great insecurities have gone and so have the rituals. We no longer fear destitution or starvation. We do not live in constant guilt over our sexual fantasies. We have no rigid class system that makes us feel inferior to others. There is a lack of formality in our lives that removes the shyness that was so often there before. Many of us do not see death at first hand. What is the price we pay for all this? Blandness. A lack of the peaks of living as well as the troughs. Sex, for example, has become disinhibited and guiltless. Young women have become as predatory as men were always. The physical pleasures of sex have become detached from our emotions. But love itself has become less urgent and less overwhelming. All the insecurities of life that used to contribute to passion are in reduced supply. The secrecy and intimacy of sex that once intensified the experience of love are less than once they were. So are the vulnerability and dependency of women and the macho denial of weakness and of emotion in men. All these features of the psychological landscape are softened. We do not need other people as once we did. We do not yearn for affection or admiration or dependency quite so much. We can stand on our own two feet in a world that is far safer, richer and fuller of opportunity for most people than it has ever been before. So love itself is now beginning to be regarded as an aberration. To show a passionate interest in another is almost considered akin to mental illness and, not unlike 'stalking', potentially a criminal offence. Even flirtation is reckoned to be politically incorrect in some circles and a form of sexual harassment. How sad!

In a desperate attempt to revive our jaded emotions, we unlock the last locked rooms of pain, sadism and disgust. Disinhibition about sex has reduced our sublimated sexual longing for beauty. So art, so-called, now tries to shock and to explore the realms of ugliness and horror. Pornography daily provokes and exhausts our lusts. Yet our largely innate capacities for disgust, squeamishness and pain still remain fairly intact. They alone provide us with the luxury of *real feeling*. (Even sadism itself, however, has been eroded. The elemental and instinctive pleasure in the control and subjugation of others was, in the past, augmented by our frustrated lusts and anger. Today, these frustrations have faded and with them has evaporated the hothouse climate in which the evil weed of sadism once flourished.) So what remains un-desensitised in our bland society? The answer is the fears of pain and death. These are the final frontiers upon which we must focus morally.

Are aggression and violence always with us? Yes. But, in my opinion, higher apparent levels of violence in modern society are the effects of reduced inhibition and not of increased anger or greater aggressive drive. Innately, we can act aggressively to protect ourselves, our property, our food sources, our partners and our families. But if these are never threatened we can go through life quite unaggressively. Violence is not a universal drive that has to be satisfied like hunger does. A contented person may never feel aggressive. Anger, however, is one cause of violence, and in almost everybody's life there are three sets of circumstances that can stimulate anger. These are, first, the *threats* just mentioned, secondly, other *insults* to our self esteem and, thirdly, *frustrations*. So if, for example, my property is threatened, or if I am personally insulted or if I cannot do what I want to do, then I may begin to feel anger – and anger sometimes leads to violence.

Anger is, of course, a perfectly natural emotion and its legitimacy should not be denied. Like its emotional cousins of joy, fear and grief it should be acknowledged and respected. There is a dangerous tendency appearing today to regard anger as profoundly disreputable. It is not. To suppress an emotion is a recipe for trouble ahead. Besides, anger can sometimes be a motive force for good. Anger at the suffering of others can provoke reforms.

As painists our concern with violence is that it often causes pain in others. It is perhaps encouraging, therefore, to realise that violence is not itself an innate drive but merely a response to circumstances. A contented society is a less violent one, and a less violent society is more contented. Most violence is not motivated by anger at all, but by compliance with a cultural norm. Soldiers usually lack anger when they kill. Ethically speaking, it is, therefore, important to ensure that society's norms are good ones.

Life in Western societies has become more affluent and, superficially at least, more contented. Yet it is also less certain. The managerial ascendancy of the 1980s and the materialism of the Thatcherite revolution in Britain has created increasing middle-class job insecurity and this in turn has made people more selfish. Long-term planning has given way to a continuous search for short-term gratifications. More people live on their own. Older professional values have given way to a more proletarian outlook. Sense of service to others has withered. Is it time for a considered reaction to these changes?

Divorce law

In some Western countries the divorce laws are deeply immoral. The concern of the state should be solely with the protection of the weak and not with normal adults who decide to stop living together.

Rule 27: In divorce law the concern of the state should be solely with the protection from suffering of children and the disabled.

In Britain, one partner can leave the other and then claim a huge financial settlement regardless of fault. For example, an idle husband with an affluent but hard-working wife can run off with another woman and force his jilted spouse to pay him hundreds of thousands of pounds, perhaps forcing her to sell her home in the process. (This happens even in the absence of children.) This situation applies regardless of the gender of the deserting spouse.

If a lodger had an affair with his landlady and then, after a few years, left to live with another woman, would a court support his claim that the landlady should give him a huge payment? If the imaginary lodger emptied his ex-lover landlady's safe before he left her, taking a few hundred thousand pounds, would the courts agree that he had a right to take it? Of course not. Then what is different about a marriage certificate? Such daylight robbery frequently occurs in cases of divorce. Does a piece of paper that hardly exists alter the whole situation? Are young people who are marrying told of the financial implications of what they are doing? This is the greatest financial risk they are ever likely to take in their lives, yet nobody seems to explain what it implies. Thus, current divorce law breaks many of the principles of justice. It can make an already painful situation even more painful for a jilted spouse by adding financial ruin to emotional injury. In other words, the law actually intensifies the pain of the maximum sufferer! Recent changes in the law as regards pensions aggravate the situation even further. To deprive one partner of much of their pension adds yet further to this monstrous injustice.

Perhaps the greatest of all faults with the current British divorce law is that it provides a strong financial incentive for husbands and wives to leave their spouses and to destroy families, thus causing great pain to children, other relatives and friends. Family life can often be poisonous. But when it works it can be the source of tremendous contentment. The active destruction of families by the state, caused by current divorce law, seems to be deeply morally wrong.

The rights of children

Everywhere the wishes of children are being overruled by adults who, allegedly, know better than do the children what is in the children's real interests. Whereas the preferences of adults (whether or not they are healthy) are usually respected, the preferences of children, for example, to watch television and play instead of going to school, are overridden. Is it surprising that, by the time a child reaches adolescence, this backlog of frustration so often erupts into rebellion? One persistent Victorian idea is that the child is wicked unless its energies are constrained. (Some of this adult attitude may emanate from a fear of children's sexuality although childish boisterousness, too, is a natural irritant that many adults want to see contained.)

What, then, should be done about the rights of children? Children are, it seems, in a very similar ethical position to that of animals. They are the weak. Adults have power over them. In Britain, children are generally far less tyrannically oppressed than they were fifty or a hundred years ago. As a result, I believe, one sees, on average, happier and better behaved children today. But there is still a tendency to deny children basic adult rights such as the freedom to choose or refuse education, to vote, or to live where and with whom they want to live. Lower levels of overall social restraint cause children and young people to lead less inhibited lives than they did half a century ago. This means that socially irritating impulses are more likely to be expressed. On the other hand, the feelings of anger and rebelliousness against adults which drive antisocial behaviour, are, overall, less intense than they used to be. So one ends up with less inhibited and less angry children who are, probably, no more tiresome on average than the children of earlier generations. On moral grounds, should this freedom for children be increased? We have a special duty of care towards children but over and above this, do we have a right to restrict their harmless liberties any more than we restrict the harmless liberties of adults? It seems hard to find rational support for this notion. Too much liberty, of course, can lead to feelings of insecurity and aimlessness and children often seem to feel happiest when they know where they stand. They suffer when they feel neglected, unloved or un-structured. One can conclude, therefore, that adults owe children a special duty of care, attention and structure.

Do we, as adults, have a right to corporally punish children? Why should we have a greater right to do this than we do to cor-porally punish adults? Indeed, in as much as adults are 'old enough to know better' the case against beating or hitting children seems even stronger. On the other hand, are we right to allow a degree of licence to children – an age of criminal responsibility for exam-ple? On the other side of this particular coin, is it morally correct to disallow children, on the grounds of age, certain adult rights to property, sex and to the ballot box? Children are better informed than ever. They matter so much to us that it is quite remarkable that among philosophers there has been so little discussion of their moral standing.

Bullying at school and work

Here is an issue that hardly presents as being difficult. Everyone can agree that bullying is wrong. There is no right to bully (al-though sadistic pleasure is undoubtedly gained by the practice) and there is no real moral conflict. What is remarkable, however, about bullying, is that it causes such intense pain and yet it is hardly recognised as a criminal offence. It should be.

It seems likely that thousands of children are bullied at school and many more thousands of adults are bullied by employers and peers at work. Yet relatively few cases are brought to court and even fewer result in serious penalties being imposed. Bullying is one of the most morally repugnant of all behaviours. It is akin to torture. The gains are purely personal and rarely are there any miti-gating excuses. Yet it is overlooked as a major ethical issue. Instead of spending much time and public money on catching safe motor-ists who exceed speed limits, marijuana smokers and minor sexual offenders the police should spend more time on the prosecution of bullies. The neglect of bullying is an example of where society has got its moral priorities wrong.

Rule 28: Any behaviour, such as bullying, which causes severe unnecessary pain should, prima facie, be an offence in law.

Employment

Although much philosophical attention, quite rightly, has been paid to civil rights and to the protection of the individual from the oppression of the state, relatively little attention is given to oppression by employers. Yet many of us spend most of our waking lives at work. It follows that the quality of our lives in general depends to a very large extent upon the quality of our lives in the workplace. Many employers, however, hardly take into account their ethical responsibilities to their work force. Despite improved employment legislation, employers too often seem concerned only with productivity and profits. People at the top of a business often suffer far less stress than those beneath them. Yet they get paid more, feel more important and enjoy the luxury of being able to make decisions.

Of course, a businessman has obligations to shareholders and to consumers. But if he does not please them the business will, ultimately, falter; so it is in his interests to please his shareholders and customers. However, his workforce is more dependent, more replaceable and more at his mercy. Furthermore, a mistreated subordinate will often suffer more than a mistreated client or customer, not only because a job takes up so much of an employee's life, but also because a job is normally the main source of her income and is one of the mainsprings of her sense of self-identity and self-esteem. Pain caused at work cannot easily be avoided or walked away from. Yet in the early twenty-first century job security has almost vanished. This feeling of insecurity in Western society is a potent source of pain. For all these reasons, and bearing in mind the principle that our first concern should always be with maximum sufferers, an employer's first moral concern, as a general rule, should be with the well-being of each of his employees.

Rule 29: In the workplace, the interests of employees should come first and then, only later, should come the interests of shareholders and consumers.

The welfare state

The welfare state is, in principle, the supreme example of applied ethics. It aims to prevent or reduce the pains of ignorance, poverty and illness. It is, surely, the greatest institutionalised achievement of human goodness. This is not the place to argue for changes in the way that the health or education services, or the provision of jobs, benefits and pensions, are administered and funded. We must not lose sight, however, of the welfare state's ultimate objective which is to reduce the suffering caused by Beveridge's five 'giant evils' of want, disease, squalor, ignorance and idleness. Many wrong turns have been taken over the years. The widespread closure of British psychiatric hospitals in the 1980s, for example, and the provision of grossly inadequate 'care in the community' have caused intense suffering for countless thousands of psychiatrically disturbed people, their families and the public at large. This great evil persists, excused by the false idea that an individual's 'freedom' from being voluntarily accommodated in a caring institution is a greater good than her happiness. In consequence, patients roam the streets, swelling the ranks of the homeless, cold, dirty and underfed. Many, out of despair, kill themselves. Occasionally, they kill or injure others. Yet idiot voices continue to argue for their freedom from the fantasised evils of a warm hospital environment. When, through neglect, such unfortunates behave sufficiently oddly or unsocially it falls to the hapless police to arrest them. They then, at colossal financial cost to society, and miserably for themselves, clog our courts and prisons.

Few people suffer more pain than the unsatisfactorily treated severely depressed. These individuals are in a living hell. They are maximum sufferers. Highly effective treatments exist but, for ideological or other reasons, these treatments in many cases are not being properly applied. To withhold such treatments (including electro-convulsive therapy if necessary) is wicked. So-called care in the community has often been a major failure and a great cruelty.

The failures of the British National Health Service are far more morally important than are most alleged failures in education. They involve the causing or permitting of the most severe forms of pain whether due to incompetence, poor administration or under funding. On the probably false assumption that they will incur electoral defeat if they raise taxes, successive British governments have failed morally on this issue. In general, of course, the emphases of health services should be upon the prevention of illness and the minimisation of suffering. Far too much emphasis is currently placed upon treatment. Often this in itself is painful. It is still true that we all have to die. Much greater resources, therefore, should be spent upon the control of pain, the elevation of mood and the general easing of the process of dying. Hospitals should be rebuilt in the style of comfortable hotels and become temples to the arts of analgesia and contentment.

Rule 30: The failure effectively to apply existing technology to treat the mentally and physically ill and to relieve their sufferings is currently one of the greatest immoralities of Western governments.

An inefficient health service can cause great suffering. The last-minute postponement of operations, for example, is a common occurrence in Britain today. But it should be recognised as an unacceptable form of cruelty. Incompetent bureaucrats responsible for such 'cat and mouse' cruelty should be charged under the criminal law.

The police

A policeman's lot is not always a happy one. But it can be, in some countries, a structured and well-paid job offering opportunities for promotion, a life full of interest, a sense of social utility and many material benefits. It is strange to me, therefore, that so few police services seem to have understood their democratic role and accountability or to have acquired even an elementary grasp of the principles of justice. Instead, reports from all over the world are of police corruption, racism and brutality. Surely there is a need to select and train the police so that they adopt standards similar to those found in other professions and even in some armed forces. If the 'wrong sort of people' tend to join the police then it is surely not beyond the ingenuity of governments to provide a remedy.

Anybody who cares about applied ethics must be concerned about the police. They have so much potential for good in society. They also have the power to do great harm. When a civilian causes a certain amount of unnecessary pain then they do wrong. When someone in authority, wearing a uniform and backed by the power of the state, causes the same amount of pain as the civilian, then their culpability is far greater. We should be able to expect our police to behave in a far better manner when they are on duty than we expect most people to behave most of the time.

A primary duty of the police is to protect the public. Undoubtedly, the British police do a very great deal of good in this respect. However, they can also cause much unnecessary pain by, for example, stopping, questioning or searching individuals who, until convicted, are presumed innocent. Much depends upon *how* these procedures are carried out. Are they done in a friendly manner or in a manner that is likely to cause fear? The police must understand that their job is to provide a service to society. They are neither a law unto themselves nor a punitive force, nor an arm of the government, nor in the employ of any class or faction. The actual position is that we, the taxpayers, employ *them* to protect *us*. Whereas some armed forces have today made the transition from seeing themselves solely as warrior/killers into becoming skilled peacekeepers, it seems to me that the police have, so far, failed to progress from seeing themselves as punitive authorities into becoming helpers and protectors. They should be social workers, albeit of a special kind. Maybe, as G. F. Newman has suggested, pink uniforms would help to change their attitude!

As a general rule, the police have great power to cause pain. Ordinary members of the public can be extremely sensitive to any sort of attention by the police. I have known a police caution for a very minor offence cause an acute psychological disturbance in a non-delinquent teenager. Heavy-handedness or minimal tolerance is highly likely to be counterproductive. It is very easy to create fear and resentment in the public mind. Because ordinary people are so apprehensive of the police, the police should be aware that the pain they can cause by 'ordinary' procedures can be disproportionate to any advantages gained. The police tend to spend too much time on issues such as the possession of marijuana, parking offences and the apprehension of fast (rather than careless) drivers, and not enough on protecting the weak from abuse. *Surely it is the job of the police to enforce those laws that relieve the pain of society's maximum sufferers.* As to deliberate wrongdoing by the police themselves (for example, corruption, racism, sexism, brutality or the rigging of evidence) then this, if proved, deserves not lesser punishment than is meted out to ordinary offenders, but far greater. The cold-blooded framing of innocent individuals by the police is deeply immoral and should be made a criminal offence that is at least as serious as most murders. I say this not only because most murders are crimes of passion and are sorely provoked, but because the framing of innocents and their false conviction necessarily involves them in a prolonged and intense suffering that is far greater than occurs in most murders. On the bright side, however, we have to remember that without the benefit of our police services, we all would be suffering from the effects of crime and disorder to a considerably greater degree than we are. The police are, and should be, the protectors of the law-abiding public. When apprehending those suspected of breaking the law the police should apply minimal force, assume the suspects are innocent until proved guilty, and observe their rights.

Due process of law

The process of prosecution itself is often very cruel. It causes intense suffering. Where a prosecution fails and the defendant is acquitted there should be a right to compensation. I have met individuals deeply scarred psychologically because they were charged with a minor offence. When acquitted nobody, except the defendant, thought much more about it. The lawyers got paid, the press had their story and the court felt self-satisfied that an innocent person had escaped punishment. But the punishment had already occurred. The punishment lasted as long as the process, and longer. The innocent defendant had suffered shame, anxiety, depression, the loss of friends, unemployment and social ostracism for months! As to remanding in custody in the case of any but the most violent of people, this practice is clearly a major breach of human rights and should at once be stopped. It is a monstrous abuse that many young people are held in prison for weeks or months before trial. Many will, anyway, be subsequently acquitted. Is this justice? It most certainly is not. (Imprisoning asylum-seekers is no better.)

On conviction, punishment is often unnecessarily harsh not only upon the offender but upon many others, particularly friends and family. Imprisonment not only makes most offenders worse, it also disrupts families and causes intense suffering to the partners, parents and children of the offender. This is quite wrong. Community service or other alternative penalties or treatments should be developed. Aspects of the criminal justice systems of the Western democracies are outdated, ineffectual and deeply immoral. They need rethinking. Prison conditions, too, perpetuated by populist politicians, are often appallingly cruel.

Crimes, also, are often given quite the wrong priorities by society. The theft of property can cause intense pain if that property belongs to an individual. If, however, it belongs to a corporation its theft may scarcely cause any pain at all. Yet such distinctions are hardly made in law. In my view, they should be. For example, the theft of gold bullion from a bank (provided no suffering is caused) is a vastly less serious offence morally than is the average act of bullying in a school yard. So the latter deserves far greater attention from the police than does the former.

Torture

The apparent increase in the use of torture by state authorities around the world is one of the most disturbing of all current trends. But can any case at all be made for torture? Are there any circumstances under which it might be justified? Of course, despots would argue that the torture of A is necessary in order to obtain information or other benefit for B. But we have agreed that the deliberate infliction of *severe* pain is never to be allowed, regardless of benefits. Then how about *slight* torture? How about imprisonment? This causes suffering. Is it, therefore, torture? Is it torture to interrogate, to lock in a cell, to deprive of luxury food? Clearly, we are on a slippery slope.

We also have to make distinctions between possible benefits. If we capture a terrorist who knows where he has imprisoned some hostage children, do we have a right to bring painful pressure upon him to tell us where they are before they starve to death? Is it justifiable to imprison such a terrorist in solitary confinement, deprive him of sleep or to stop his supply of good food, until he tells us, or is it permissible to go far further and, for example, to subject him to painful electric shocks? The possible benefits (saving the lives of children) seem so great in this case. On the other hand, if the information we want is merely the whereabouts of another terrorist then this seems less persuasive.

We have to be very careful of our footing here because we are on at least two slippery slopes – concerning not only the degree of torture inflicted but also the degree of benefit to be gained from it. Utilitarians must go along with the use of torture in some circumstances while strict Rightists may oppose it absolutely. Are there, then, any rules we can suggest, based upon the principles of painism? Can I play devil's advocate by finding any circumstances at all under which duress or torture could be ethically permitted? We already have the rule that it is *never* permissible to inflict *severe* pain. Is it, then, ever permissible to inflict moderate pain? Or slight pain? This is the same problem, ethically speaking, as faces the animal experimenter. One difference is that our convicted terrorist has already been found guilty of an offence. Let us say that there is no official doubt about the facts. He is not an innocent. Does this in itself permit us to do to him what we would not be permitted to do to an innocent? Is innocence relevant? I think it may be, provided the terrorist has been found to be guilty by due process of law and if the law itself is fair and allows subsequent duress upon him. If (to take the worst case) our terrorist has been shown to be guilty of kidnapping children and if the court decides that he, and only he, can reveal information that will, *beyond all reasonable doubt,* save the children, then the court could permit duress. Of course, we are concerned primarily with reducing the suffering of the child who is suffering most. The pain of starving to death must be estimated. It is surely likely to be more painful than being placed in solitary confinement but it is probably less painful than being roasted alive on a grid iron. Would we ever be justified in causing the terrorist, guilty or not, more pain than any of the children are suffering? *The future development of applied ethics will depend to a large extent upon the development of techniques to measure and compare the intensity of pains.*

A convict being in a position to stop 'ongoing' pain is, of course, most unusual. I suppose that in at least 99 per cent of cases before the courts these special conditions do not obtain. The only possible justification for authorising duress is in order to gain, beyond all reasonable doubt, a reduction in the suffering of maximum sufferers. But the possibility of such trade-offs should be faced. Inflicting duress arbitrarily, or in order merely to punish an individual or for political or selfish gains, or as an example to others is total anathema. Generally, torture must be regarded as the very worst offence of all. The deliberate infliction of pain as a means to a political end is, prima facie, very wrong indeed. Torture is the greatest of all evils (*see* Rule 16).

Political theory

Political theory has largely addressed the question of *justice*. Political philosophers have tried to set up principles of justice and have tended to assert that justice is the prime virtue. The work of John Rawls, for example, which dominates the subject today, is much concerned with the relationship between justice, liberty and equality. As we have seen above (pp. 20ff.) Rawls postulates that if we did not know what position we would hold in a society (for example, what status, gender or race – and I would add, species), then from behind this 'veil of ignorance' we would play safe by choosing to arrange that society in such a way that, first, 'each person is to have an equal right to the most extensive total system of equal basic liberties compatible with a similar system of liberty for all' (this has been called Rawls' Liberty Principle) and, secondly, that 'social and economic inequalities are to be arranged so that they are both: (a) to the greatest benefit of the least advantaged' (called the Difference Principle) and '(b) attached to offices and positions open to all under conditions of fair equality of opportunity' (called the Fair Opportunity Principle).[3] Rawls ranks these three principles so that liberty comes first followed by fair opportunity and then the difference principle.

There is something strange about Rawls' starting point. How can the hypothetical choices of those behind a veil of ignorance determine the nature of justice? Is it justice they are choosing, or are they calculating their self-interest? If such choices are so important, why not set social scientists to carry out an actual experiment to ascertain the facts? Rawls may claim that this is only a theoretical exercise and not real psychology but then why does he attach so much importance to 'choices', 'ignorance' and 'rationality' – these are, after all, *psychological* concepts. Rawls assumes that rational people always want liberty, opportunity and money and that they show no interest in the condition of others. I would doubt the latter point.

From the point of view of painism and, indeed, Utilitarianism, Rawls' emphasis upon justice, equality and liberty, seems to miss the point. These conditions are merely means to an end. They are only stepping stones to contentment. They are desirable because, so it is believed, they will lead to happiness – or at least to the reduction of suffering. Children are extremely sensitive to issues of justice – the fair or equal treatment of siblings by parents is almost universally a matter of family sensitivity and any deviations are likely to affect the formation of personality and the behaviour of family members. In childhood, too, we become very sensitised to the question of liberty because, almost inevitably, the freedoms of children are, to some extent, frustrated by adult rules and discipline. Feeling restricted is unpleasant. But, then, so also is the feeling of total freedom – or, at least, it can be. People will not *always* choose complete freedom, and especially if they have had some painful experience of it. Yet if Rawls is trying to produce a picture of the 'good' society, he may not have entirely failed. He says that such a society will contain a high level of liberty, equality of opportunities and some inequalities that benefit, to the greatest extent, the least advantaged. If, according to the principles of painism, this has the effect of reducing the sufferings of the greatest sufferers then this seems to be on the right lines. In games theory terms both Rawls' theory and painism tend to take a 'maximin' approach – that is to say they try to ensure that the worst possible outcome is as good as possible – we 'maximise the minimum'. Utilitarianism will part company here – it seeks merely to maximise the aggregation of benefits, or, in special versions of Utilitarianism, to make the *average* position in society as good as possible.

The maximin approach has been criticised as being rather boring. It avoids risk-taking. A possible compromise solution involves permitting inequality and introducing a 'safety net' so that however much risk is taken, or however great the inequalities are in society, the worst off are always protected from total destitution by such safety nets as the welfare state and a minimum wage. This, too, seems an attractive proposition for painists.

Robert Nozick has contested Rawls' theory from a right wing libertarian perspective. One of the problems with arguments about liberty is that freedom can refer to the freedom to act in entirely different ways – freedom to love and to care on one hand, or freedom to oppress and exploit, on the other, for example. If liberalism is about the freedom of the individual to self-expression and self-fulfilment then libertarianism is about the freedom of the market and the maximisation of the individual's economic rights. Both liberals and libertarians can champion the rights of the individual against the power of the state. Nozick, for example, denies that the state has the right to levy taxes against the property rights of the individual. Taxes, Nozick claims, are similar to forced labour – if we pay 25 per cent of our income in tax then this means, in effect, that 25 per cent of our working week is unpaid. Taxation, then, is like slavery. Nozick concludes that Rawls' two main principles of liberty and difference (which includes the redistribution of property through taxation) are basically incompatible. Certainly, taxation restricts the liberty of the better-off but if this means that benefits will be redistributed to the less well off then this is increasing *their* liberties. It is a familiar conflict of rights. We are, in theory at least, causing pain (through taxation) to A in order to reduce the pain of B (e.g., the patient who benefits from free medical treatment). Provided this procedure conforms to our proposed rules (*see* particularly my Rules 7–11) then it is acceptable. But how much of the tax we pay is actually spent, for example, on reducing the pain of maximum sufferers who are not human (almost zero), or on reducing pain rather than increasing pleasure?

Rule 31: The infliction of pain through taxation is not justified unless the revenue is effectively spent on the reduction of the severe pains of the worst-off, i.e., the maximum sufferers of all ages, sexes, races and species.

Painism certainly champions the rights of the individual against those of the state. The state itself is not painient. So there is no such thing as 'the general will' or 'the general good'. They are fictions. There is only the suffering of individuals. Perhaps there is too much talk of justice, equality and liberty in political philosophy and not enough about suffering. It is suffering that matters morally and although justice, equality and liberty are usually correlated with the reduction of suffering this is not always the case. A painist looks beyond justice, equality and liberty to a more fundamental reality. How the principles of equality, liberty, justice and democracy interact is highly interesting, although not central to painism. Ronald Dworkin, for example, asserts that these principles are mutually consistent.[4] Maybe this is because all tend to correlate negatively with individual suffering. There are, however, instances where this does not work. In politics hard choices have to be made between them. Too much freedom is sometimes painful. Equality and justice (for all) will inhibit individual liberty, and so on. Dworkin is anxious to assert the ideal of equality but here the obvious conflict is with individual merit: if A works far harder than B, are you going to take away his earnings and give them to B? How about 'affirmative action' (i.e., giving special advantages to disadvantaged sections of the community)? Is it fair to discriminate in favour of certain traditionally downtrodden groups? In my view it is not fair if this means that others of higher merit (in terms of skill or labour, for example) suffer a disadvantage by not getting jobs and so on. Nor do I believe that it is meaningful to argue that affirmative action is justified in order to compensate for past injustice to certain ethnic groups. The past is the past. Pain is in the present and not the past.

Rule 32: We must, as painists, be concerned with the sufferings of individuals now and in the future and not with the past pains of individuals who may or may not be still with us.

There are two sides to human nature – the selfish and the compassionate. Hobbes somewhat overlooked the psychological reality of our capacity to feel compassion for others. Among political philosophers, it was Jean-Jacques Rousseau who argued that compassion exists as a powerful restraint on our aggressive and acquisitive drives. He was right. It is on this faculty of compassion that our laws should be based and our world order constructed. Plato believed that states should be ruled only by those who are experts in ruling. Yes, the administration should be done by administrative experts but the *direction* of government should be decided by those who can determine what will most reduce the pains of the maximum sufferers. Democracy is an approximation to this. Today, the old democratic procedures should be largely superseded by opinion polls and focus groups. These, as they become more scientific, will determine far more accurately what it is that people actually *want*. They will be able to discern the difference between what people genuinely desire and what they think they ought to say that they desire. They will be able to distinguish between genuine wants and pseudo-altruistic answers. In a new democratic system the questions would have to be determined partly by a semi-independent agency with strong legal backing, and partly by the electorate itself. Increasing political apathy (the product of cynicism and contentment) means that fewer and fewer people vote at elections. This is dangerous. To get around this problem, voting and/or the answering of official opinion polling could be made obligatory. In Britain we do not yet live in a democracy. We have a system where a minority of voters can elect governments. So we need some system of proportional representation. Using modern electronic technology every home could have a voting button. This would allow governments to consult the electors far more often and on a wide range of issues. Those failing to vote when required could easily be tracked down and interviewed. Instead of the voter going to the polling station the pollster comes to the voter. There is, indeed, a case for bringing democracy far more into our daily lives – for example, into our relationships within the family, with our doctors and employers. Democracy, however, can slow decision taking and this in itself can be painfully irritating. Maybe this sort of delay can now be avoided by the appropriate use of modern technology. There is no point, after all, in applying democracy to our lives if this causes more suffering than it alleviates.

The problems of democracy

Democracy, like justice, equality and liberty, is only a means to an end – and that end is the reduction of the pains of the maximum sufferers. But how do ordinary people know what actually will make them happy or reduce their pains? And what about the sufferings of minorities, especially if these are the maximum sufferers? Let us consider this accusation: that the chief fault in democracy is that the majority can overrule the interests of minorities. Clearly, true democracy requires the protection of minorities. Indeed, it requires the protection of individuals. The liberty of the individual to think and to do as they please, *provided that they cause no suffering to others*, must be protected. This does not give a charter to minority groups such as rapists, paedophiles, serial killers, burglars or to those who cruelly hunt animals because, clearly, such people are acting in such a way as to cause pain to others. But it does give protection to those with eccentric but harmless hobbies, unpopular opinions and peculiar beliefs. John Stuart Mill was, rightly, concerned to prevent the 'tyranny of the majority' but he also stressed the state's duty to stop 'domestic tyrants' from oppressing children, animals and other individuals weaker than themselves. Is it just a question of balance? Mill urged that minorities should be represented in Parliament, but even here they could be outvoted. So how *can* minorities be protected? How much power should the state have over individuals? Mill rejected anarchy – 'all that makes existence valuable to anyone', he wrote, 'depends on the reinforcement of restraints upon the action of other people'.[5] We may, said Mill, interfere with the liberty of adults, but *only* to prevent harm, or threat of harm, to others. Why, then, we may ask, do we still have laws against incest, prostitution (soliciting) and voluntary euthanasia? According to painism such laws should be done away with if they are causing more pain to individuals than they are reducing.

There is another great threat to democracy and that is the corrupting role of money. Money donations to political parties should be completely outlawed. In the USA money makes a mockery of democracy. How can politics be genuinely concerned with the rights of the individual, particularly of the weakest and poorest, when a few rich individuals and institutions are funding the system? In as much as parties need money for internal administration, this should be provided only by the state. It is certainly wrong that some parties should be able to finance far more election advertising than others can afford.

The twenty-first century may see the growing power of corporations and large international bodies. So far these have largely escaped the democratisation that has tamed domestic governments. The power of international commercial companies and global organisations such as the World Trade Organisation (WTO), the World Bank, the OECD and the International Monetary Fund (IMF) needs to be tempered by applied ethics. New legal institutions to counter them need to be established – international courts of law, and an international police, all ultimately under a reformed and effective United Nations (UN). In my view, too many of the global organisations lack any morality. They act like giant psychopaths on the world stage. They need to be morally trained and restrained.

The final problem for democracy today is the power of the media. The media are *not* democratic and have far more power over voting behaviour than they care to admit. Governments are made and destroyed by the unelected media. This would hardly matter if all newspapers and other media constantly told the truth and adopted an unbiased and rational approach. But they do not. Instead, we have a tabloid press that constantly and deliberately distorts. It mocks the good news and exaggerates the bad. Instead of calmness and reason we are fed sensationalism and hysteria. The news is personalised and trivialised. Dull facts are not allowed to spoil good stories. The media intrude upon the privacy of their victims and even quite intelligent journalists grow to believe in their own absurd distortions to the extent that some can no longer tell the truth from falsehood. The audience, too, even though many know that 'you cannot believe what you read in the newspapers', still do precisely that. The media who are undoubtedly the great guardians of freedom have also become the great destroyers. They are the most serious sickness of our free and democratic society.

Increasingly, we suffer from government by the media. Their conduct cannot be considered to be morally acceptable. Ministers who commit relatively minor mistakes are forced to resign – their peccadilloes hysterically exaggerated as major corruption by media that are themselves often morally corrupt and blind. What a disgrace that a handful of vindictive newspapers can destroy political careers without any due process or right of appeal. The public are dangerously and corruptingly tricked into believing that most national politicians are corrupt. This breeds a self-fulfilling cynicism about politics. The media scrutiny of politicians in modern democracies has become so intense that no aspiring politician, motivated as many are, merely to try to make the world a better place, can afford to joke, to give assistance to others or to behave sexually, without fear of 'exposure' and damnation for some alleged offence. Are the media guilty of projecting their own human failings on to the politicians? The media have such a potential for doing good. Yet, too often, they neglect it and resort instead to destructive sensationalism.

As for the electronic media, especially film and television, they show a fascination with violence. Almost certainly this encourages violence in society. To portray the heroes of a narrative as being callous, insensitive, macho or violent is likely to encourage others to imitate them. Violence on the screen is the real pornography of our age. The portrayal of sex can bring pleasure to millions whereas the promotion of violence can only lead, in the longer term, to suffering. Governments have failed adequately to restrict the television and film industries as regards their portrayal of violence, and they should do so. If any portrayal of violence provokes even one act of unjust violence then it is wrong.

Sins of commission and omission

How far should we go out of our way to do good? Is it sufficient merely to avoid causing pain to others as and when the occasion arises in our daily lives? Or are we morally required to search for pains in order to reduce them, however out of sight or far away they may be? Peter Singer has cited the issue of world poverty (along with our treatment of nonhuman animals and how we handle life and death decisions in medicine) as one of the areas where he hopes there will be moral breakthroughs in the twenty-first century.[6] He argues that 'we need to take responsibility for all the effects of our actions – and for the effects of our indifference as well'. People who are dying of hunger or of easily treatable diseases may be thousands of miles away from where I live. But this does not let me off the moral hook. *Distance alone makes no difference to suffering.* Singer condemns those who live a luxurious and profligate lifestyle while not significantly contributing to helping the poor of the world. I concur. We have responsibility not only for our actions but also for what we could have prevented.

Maybe because we feel it is beyond our power significantly to improve the lot of the distant poor or because we feel the situation is being dealt with by governments or large charities, we try to assuage our consciences. Yet, on television, we can see maximum sufferers dying of disease and starvation and suffering from political tyranny and natural disasters. This is an example of where the media have done well. Yet their actions are inconsistent. When a special crisis is highlighted by the media then the response from affluent individuals in the West is often generous.

Perhaps governments themselves should make it easier for busy people to show compassion on a global scale. Perhaps the media should be *required* to keep us consistently informed of tyrannies and disasters, and there could be government global aid collecting boxes on street corners with regular progress bulletins on television on how help is being provided. We live in a world that is commercially, politically and culturally increasingly global. *Our ethics should be global also.* We cannot all be saints but we should try to reduce the pain of others, however distant.

Rule 33: We have an obligation to try to reduce the pains of others, wherever they are, and however the pains have been caused.

An ethical foreign policy

For centuries nations have conducted trade and warfare internationally. Now, in the twenty-first century we are entering a period when nations and individuals are increasingly trying to do good in distant countries. The nineteenth century saw much harm and not a little good done by imperialists and the twentieth century saw the birth of the United Nations. Currently, in my view, the United Nations is wrongly structured, underfunded and poorly run; while to its eternal shame the great country that should give it unequivocal support, the United States, fails to do so. Yet the United Nations is beginning to disseminate some moral order in the world. Acting under United Nations resolutions military interventions to protect ethnic minorities and to curb the excesses of dictators have been partially successful in Bosnia, Kosovo, Kuwait and elsewhere. There have also been obvious failures. British troops have done particularly well in developing and applying the difficult skills of peacekeeping, while special forces have excelled in the courageous arrest of wanted war criminals and their transportation to face charges at the International Tribunal in The Hague. Such developments mark welcome progress in the application of international law and ethics. Most morally significant of all was the arrest of General Augusto Pinochet in London in 1998 on charges of torture and murder issued by a Spanish judge. The British judiciary overthrew Pinochet's claims of immunity and, at a stroke, hugely advanced the application of international ethics. No dictator in the future will be able to believe that what he does in his own fiefdom will necessarily escape international censure. Perhaps some political prisoners somewhere have already been spared torture or execution because a tyrant has been concerned that his actions might prevent him, at some time in the future, from visiting London to do his Christmas shopping. Let us hope so!

Yet the moral approach of the 1990s was, sometimes, a little strange. Attempts, for example, to return locally hated Serbian refugees to their old homes in Kosovo were obviously doomed to fail and, in the process, caused huge additional suffering. The partition of such troubled states into separate ethnic entities is the only practical solution. Clinging to the idea that anything that looks like 'ethnic cleansing' is worse than rape, terror, death and torture is clearly absurd. Such things are morally far worse than relocation to alternative accommodation.

The movement of refugees across the globe terrifies the governments of affluent states to which such people seek to travel. The treatment of immigrants – who are often people escaping dire suffering of one sort or another – is itself often unjust and cruel. Among such immigrants, surely, are many maximum sufferers. These people deserve comfort and hospitality. Instead, they far too frequently receive callous and arrogant bureaucracy, detention and rejection.

Many have questioned the right of the United Nations to 'interfere' with the internal behaviours of governments, particularly democratically elected ones. Yet, clearly, there is an overriding right. The sovereignty of nation states – and their right to behave badly – can no longer be accepted without moral question. There has been a confusion of the rights of a state with the rights of a person. But persons are quite different in that they are painient individuals. States are not, in themselves, painient, so their autonomy is less of an issue. The opposition by the USA to the establishment of a permanent international court to deal with issues such as war crimes, is itself morally indefensible.

Rule 34: When a state is unjustly causing severe suffering to individuals (whether these individuals are inside or outside that state) then we, the world community, have a duty to interfere.

The idea of the just war

Various moral principles to justify war have been developed in Europe over the centuries as a middle course between total pacifism and unbridled militarism. These have been based upon self-defence and the rescue of another country from aggression. Few attempts have been made to justify barefaced aggression itself. Arguments have centred upon whether self-defence can include defence against a threat (as well as an actual attack) and whether it is morally permissible to wage pre-emptive war. Two sets of arguments have developed, one dealing with the justification for going to war (*jus ad bellum*) and the other with the actual conduct of war (*jus in bello*). Let us first consider *jus ad bellum*. Various principles have been proposed for the so-called just recourse to war. These include just cause, proportionality, right intention, prospects of success, last resort and legitimate authority. A preoccupation with the first principle, just cause, may have encouraged wars in the past. Indeed, as Jonathan Glover has suggested, it is hard to believe that more than an insignificant number of wars throughout history have been morally justified.[7] It is easy for fanatics to be convinced by their own arguments and in most wars most participants, on all sides, have believed in the righteousness of their own causes. Most ordinary Germans, for example, believed that the Second World War was a justified defence of Germany and the civilised world. There is, rarely, in such cases, an impartial judge. Does the United Nations effectively and justly fulfil this role? Not always, but it is surely a step in the right direction. But what, approximately, constitutes 'just cause'? In modern times this phrase has been interpreted to mean either 'self-defence' or 'the defence of another state against unjust attack'. Does this include resistance against an attack that has already occurred, maybe years previously? Or preemptive resistance to an attack that has not yet occurred but is perceived to be threatened? If the principle of self-defence is permitted then pre-emptive strikes must be recognised as being, in some circumstances, the most effective form of self-defence. A. J. Coates[8] has concluded that the equation of the just war with a defensive war has become acceptable. 'Without an injury received or threatened, no war can be justified', he argues, 'in that sense all just wars are reactive or defensive wars, and all unjust wars are wars of aggression.' The United Nations to an extent concurs by endorsing 'the inherent right of individual or collective self-defence if an armed attack occurs'.

How, then, about the other traditional principles of launching a just war – proportionality, right intention, prospects for success, last resort and legitimate authority? I would like to take *proportionality* and *last resort* together as both being of particular interest to painist theory and allocate the others to a more pragmatic category. Waging war as a last resort only when other more peaceful methods have been tried and found to fail, seems obviously acceptable. Care, however, should be taken to avoid any delay that increases suffering. Proportionality in recourse to war seems to involve calculations as to whether war is the only possible response, whether the injury received is sufficiently serious to provoke war, and whether the resultant benefits of war will outweigh the resultant evils. The 'fog of war' makes such calculations extremely difficult. However, in calculating the outcomes, as a painist, I would not be impressed by the quantity of individuals who suffer (on each side) but by the *intensity* of their sufferings. This is an important distinction. Head counts or body counts are not the proper basis, morally speaking, for making a decision on whether or not to wage war. I therefore propose the following rules:

Rule 35: Simply counting the number of dead or wounded on both sides of a dispute, or indeed counting the number of people to be defended, are not factors to be taken into account when deciding matters of jus ad bellum *in the declaration of war. It is, instead, the maximum levels of individual suffering on both sides that must be taken into account.*

Rule 36: Recourse to war, because it inevitably causes severe suffering, must only be a matter of last resort.

Rule 37: Recourse to war is only permissible in self-defence or in the defence of others from unjust attack where this attack is causing, or has recently caused, severe pain and, preferably in the opinion of an impartial judge, threatens to do so again.

As to *right intention* and *legitimate authority* I will only treat these briefly. If an attack is unjust I am morally required to defend the victim regardless of anyone else's 'authority'. Nevertheless it seems highly desirable that a just war should be supported by the widest and most impartial authority available. Such is the United Nations. As to intentions, right or wrong, these are of little moral relevance. It is the *consequences* of actions that matter morally speaking although, of course, in deciding to wage war I should be motivated to put those consequences right by reducing the sufferings of maximum sufferers. It is never right to wage war merely for some principle of punishment or revenge.

*Rule 38: In all calculations of the justness of recourse to war (and its conduct) the consequences upon **all** painients should be taken into account whether these are local or distant, present or future, or human or nonhuman.*

Rules for the conduct of war (*jus in bello*) seem even more relevant to painism. Although war is 'an act of violence pushed to its utmost bounds' (Clausewitz) it is nevertheless imperative that moral rules are applied in such conditions. War intensifies the need for morality, it does not suspend it.

The theory of *jus in bello* usually consists of three principles – the principle of *proportionality*, the principle of *minimal force* and the principle of *discrimination*. Proportionality requires that the bad consequences of war should not outweigh its predicted good consequences. In painist terms this means that the maximum levels of suffering caused by the war should not outweigh the greatest amounts of individual suffering reduced. So it would be wrong, for example, to torture a prisoner of war or cause agony to an enemy soldier by using a cruel chemical weapon in order to stop a fairly peaceful military occupation. Here, the agony of one individual outweighs the milder suffering (by being peacefully occupied) caused to many. Again, ethical decisions in war should not be swayed by the quantity of individuals (e.g., refugees) affected, but by the degree or intensity of individual suffering.

Modern warfare increasingly opens up the prospect not only of the use of accurate and selective weaponry but also of more humane weaponry. After all, the objective, militarily speaking, is to incapacitate, not necessarily to wound or kill. The use of weapons that temporarily incapacitate without causing great distress (for example, by the use of mass anaesthetics, tranquillisers or other devices that temporarily confuse, blind or paralyse painlessly) should be seen as the way forward for the future. The greater emphasis upon the disablement or destruction of military equipment (tanks, aircraft, guns etc.) rather than personnel, seen in recent wars such as in Kosovo, Bosnia and even the Gulf, is much to be welcomed morally speaking. Knocking out the enemy's hardware rather than targeting his troops should be an accepted priority.

Troops without weapons or provisions can usually be persuaded to surrender.

The principle of *minimal force* means not using violence in excess of what is necessary to achieve an objective. This is clearly morally desirable to the extent that the level of violence tends to be positively correlated with the level of suffering caused to maximum sufferers. Again the emphasis should be upon causing less pain to individuals rather than in reducing the quantity of enemy personnel affected. Both the principles of minimal force and proportionality are morally correct although in practice, if poorly applied, they can have the opposite effect to that intended. For example, not using sufficient force may actually prolong a conflict thus prolonging the suffering of individuals. This danger needs to be recognised and allowed for. Sometimes the mere threat of ruthless or overwhelming force can produce a desirable result which reduces maximum suffering, not only to one's own troops but to the enemy's as well.

Conduct after a battle is also of great moral importance. Upholding the rights of the vanquished as well as the victors is crucial. A generous and humane attitude towards prisoners not only reduces their suffering as individuals but may be the first steps towards reconciliation and a genuine peace.

The third principle of conduct in war is the principle of discrimination. This refers to the identification of legitimate targets. Should distinctions be made between combatants and noncombatants or between the innocent and the guilty? How do we judge guilt and innocence in the heat of battle? Just because someone is wearing a suit in an office rather than a uniform in a tank this does not prove their innocence – he or she may be the minister for war! Many soldiers in uniform may be conscripts who have been forced to fight. How does a uniform confer guilt? After all, dictators have often put their political enemies in the front lines of battle. Yet, clearly, for very practical reasons, we have to target the person who is shooting at us or who, to the best of our knowledge, we *believe* is shooting at us or is about to do so. Generally, though, of course, the civilian population should not be targeted. Unarmed soldiers or armed combatants who pose no threat or who appear to be wishing to surrender should be spared. Indeed, the helpless civilian and the prisoner of war should be extended every possible humane consideration. These are some of the traditional tests of civilisation and they should be respected. If there is to be a shift in our moral discriminations for the future conduct of wars it is in two directions:

Rule 39: The prime targets of war should be military equipment rather than military personnel.

Rule 40: Those who have caused or ordered an unjust war should themselves become prime targets.

This last rule means that far greater efforts should be made to target individual dictators, political leaders and top generals. These are the people who should be captured or, if this cannot be done, killed. There has, for far too long, been a taboo on the targeting and assassination of belligerent political leaders. Ideally, they should be given the benefit of being captured and tried according to the principles of international law and under United Nations direction. The knowledge by warmongers, whether terrorist warlords or heads of state, that their lives will be at risk if they wage unjust war, would act as a powerful deterrent. This is where the use of special forces comes in. Knowing that their lives and liberties will be at risk, even after a successful war, and perhaps for years, will make war-instigators far more circumspect. We are entering a period of internationalism, and international policing is part of this. Warrants for the arrest of the world's dictators should be issued and means developed to affect arrests or at least to threaten them. This has already been done in the case of Serbian and other Balkan war criminals. The practice needs to be refined and extended. These are the people who have given the orders that have led to so much suffering. It is not the foot soldier who should be targeted, it is his leader, often far from the battlefront, whose safe domestic life needs to be jeopardised.

Further ethical and psychological aspects of war

The just war is an example, and probably the most devastating example, of applying the moral 'trade-off' (*see* chapter 2). We cause pain to A in order to reduce the pain of B. In order to stop Serbians persecuting Kosovars we bomb Serbia. We cause pain to Serbians in order to reduce the pain of Kosovars. Is this justifiable? Yes, provided that the suffering of Kosovan individuals was severe and provided there was no other less violent way and provided the bombing was likely to succeed in having the desired effect. Eventually it did. This is consistent with the rules of thumb already agreed in Chapter 2, and most of the principles of a just war. Of course, it is very difficult, in practice, to calculate the degrees of suffering experienced on both sides. We can, however, surely assume that in war the sufferings of individuals are likely to be extreme. I believe we should proceed on this assumption.

One of the problems arising from the Kosovo episode was the effects of attacking from a distance. So great was NATO's desire to protect its own troops – which it did with quite remarkable success – that it used long-range methods such as cruise missiles and bombing from a height of 15,000 feet. These tactics necessarily increased the harm done to 'innocent' civilians in Serbia. This concerns the principle of discrimination. It is rarely possible to determine innocence or guilt during a war by due process of law and a properly conducted trial. It is especially difficult from 15,000 feet. Guilt in war, anyway, remains an ambiguous concept. We can say that NATO did not *intend* to harm innocent civilians but, of course, everybody realised that some, inevitably, would be hurt. Yet it is the consequences of action that matter morally and not the intentions of the agent. One can certainly question NATO's application of the principle of discrimination. Nevertheless, NATO's involvement in stopping the Serbian atrocities in Kosovo (however few cases there were) remains in, most respects, an example of a just war. After a war efforts should, of course, be made to create a peace and to restore a good quality of life for the survivors. This includes an obligation upon the victors to assist in the removal of deadly debris such as mines, unexploded bombs and toxic pollution such as that left by the use of depleted uranium warheads.

Machismo and other psychological matters

Psychologically speaking, there are several important principles involved in conducting war and in explaining why ordinary people can bring themselves to kill in war. The first is that we are innate warriors and this is deep in our genes. For most of us, most of our lives, our warrior/killer instincts are suppressed and contained. When they are liberated, ordinary men and women can be shocked to discover how easily and *enjoyably* they become killers. Secondly, the almost universal cult of machismo, which teaches that every man (and sometimes women, too) must be brave and hard, encourages warlike rather than compassionate and gentle action. Thirdly, we all tend to obey orders and most of us will do morally terrible things if authority tells us to do so. This fact has been demonstrated repeatedly by Stanley Milgram and other psychologists. If we find ourselves part of an evil culture – such as in Serbia or in Nazi Germany – then about 60 per cent of us will, without much question, conform to it. Fourthly, it is easy for generals at a distance to give orders that have such horrific consequences that if they personally witnessed them at close quarters they would be appalled. One of the effects of distance is that it makes war easier. Distance reduces the restrictive effects of fear and of our equally innate instincts of squeamishness and compassion at the sight of others' suffering. These are less likely to be stimulated at a distance. The moral implications that could be applied are that:

(1) The cult of machismo, so commonly encouraged in sports, in schools, on television and in literature should be itself suppressed.

(2) The dangers of obedience to authority, as well as its advantages (e.g., the respect for law), should be explained in our schools and the psychological research of Milgram and others discussed.

(3) All wars should be officially televised and their awful consequences, in terms of pain and distress, should be required viewing for the generals and politicians who are in charge. These people should also be made to visit the front lines.

The arms trade

The arms trade poses particular ethical problems. Is there ever any justification for selling a gun? Perhaps if one can be certain that the gun will be used only in self-defence or in a just war. But as this guarantee is, in practical terms, impossible, then guns should never be sold. Ideally, we need a global police force under the control of the United Nations. Perhaps they alone should have weapons. Unarmed police, for domestic purposes, provided they are well trained, can do a very good job in maintaining public order. The selling of weapons, whether to individuals over the counter or by governments to other governments, should cease entirely. A military weapon is an instrument of torture. Torture is wrong. There can be no guarantees that a weapon will never be used immorally.

In terms of practical politics, however, there are difficulties. Until there is a properly enforced global control of *all* weapons then the situation is awkward. If a responsible country refuses to sell weapons to another country then the latter may get them from somewhere else, perhaps from a less responsible source, who will then have influence over the purchaser. Perhaps, until global arms control is a reality, governments should only *loan* arms to another government, and under a United Nations permit that requires certain moral standards of the recipient, for example, the respect for human rights. Other items of trade, particularly when sold to less developed nations, also need to be controlled on ethical grounds – not only instruments of torture and oppression such as whips, shackles and electric police batons, but also second-rate, dangerous or experimental types of medication and other possibly harmful consumer products.

Terrorism

If terrorism is defined as the use of violence (other than by a state) to achieve a particular political objective, then its ethics is similar to that of just war and it must, at the very least, meet all the same criteria. According to painism, however, the aggregation of pains and pleasures across individuals is not allowable. This reduces very considerably the justification for violence. To use extreme violence in order to reduce lesser violence is dubious, to say the least. To cause pain (even to one individual) greater than the individual pain to be alleviated is wrong. Thus, to cause grievous and agonising injury by throwing a bomb, for example, is grossly out of proportion to the painful sense of injustice experienced by any individual who feels (e.g., ethnically) discriminated against in the ordinary (non-violent) meaning of the term. The latter experience, although painful, is in no way as painful as the pains caused by a bomb. Thus terrorism, in this context, even if it is believed to be a fight for freedom, is not justified.

Sport

Sport fulfils many of the psychological functions of war. Various sports have spread around the world in the last fifty to a hundred years, often as unsung British exports. They bring tremendous joy and sorrow to millions. If, as seems likely, they are releasing certain warlike tensions relatively harmlessly then they seem morally excellent. But there is surely a danger that they may also have an opposite effect by encouraging the cult of machismo and by increasing international rivalries and tensions. Machismo – the cult of the so-called masculine virtues of toughness and stoicism – causes a huge amount of suffering in the world. Men (and increasingly women) are encouraged to suppress sympathy and cultivate a hard and callous approach to the sufferings of other humans and nonhumans. The old knightly version – which valued mercy and protectiveness – had its moral advantages. All too easily machismo can degenerate into loutishness and cruelty. Do we need it?

The proper and just conduct of sporting contests and the effective control of hooligan supporters seem to be morally necessary restraints. Sports need to be encouraged as the humane alternative to war, not as a source of grievance and hostility. The international regulation of sport needs to be based more firmly upon ethical principles.

Human rights

One of the most important aspects of an ethical foreign policy is the consideration of human rights. Various international human rights agreements have been formulated over the years and agreed by the United Nations, the Council of Europe, the Organisation for Security and Cooperation in Europe (OSCE) and other bodies. In 1976 two UN Covenants came into force. The International Covenant on Economic, Social and Cultural Rights proposed the rights to work; an adequate standard of living; education; social security; the highest attainable health care standards; to form and join trade unions and participate in cultural life. The International Covenant on Civil and Political Rights promulgated the rights to freedom from torture or cruel, inhuman or degrading treatment; from slavery; of movement; from arbitrary expulsion; of thought and religion; of association, including trade union membership; of expression. Other rights are to privacy, equality before the law, peaceful assembly, to take part in the conduct of public affairs, and liberty. These 19 rights clearly overlap with each other. There are also UN Covenants which deal with more specific rights including the political and other rights of women; the elimination of racial discrimination; the status of refugees and stateless persons; the prevention of torture; the abolition of slavery and forced labour; the prevention and punishment of genocide; the right to collective bargaining and the freedom of association.

The Council of Europe's Convention for the Protection of Human Rights and Fundamental Freedoms covers the rights to life, liberty and a fair trial; freedom of thought, conscience and religion; freedom of expression, including freedom of the press; freedom of peaceful assembly and association, including the right to join a free trade union; the right to justice, including the right to have a sentence reviewed by a higher tribunal; the right to marry and have a family; and the prohibition of torture and inhuman or degrading treatment. Again, many of these (approximately 15) legal rights overlap with the 19 UN proposals. One or two are, arguably, additional, e.g., the rights to fair trial, freedom of press, sentence review, marriage, and family. Taken together, these 20 to 30 human rights, agreed by the United Nations or by the Council of Europe, constitute a formidable body of law. None seem blatantly inconsistent with ethical theory. Some are concerned with specific behaviours and others are more general. Most are *active* rights to act in certain ways (e.g., marry, peacefully assemble or express opinions) but many are *passive* (e.g., not to be tortured, enslaved or discriminated against). In law it may be desirable to list specific cases. However, by doing so any omissions that are not covered by the law become more significant. It can be seen that many of the issues dealt with as applied ethics in this chapter are not emphasised by the UN and European instruments: for example, abortion, euthanasia, the ethics of war, sexual behaviour, the care of the elderly, health care, environmental protection, divorce, bullying, police conduct, genetic engineering, or the protection of animals. Some of these are covered in other international agreements and some are not. Maybe it is time that these were all included and given headline status.[9]

In applied ethics so much depends on how laws are drafted and enforced. Anyone who has had dealings with the legal profession will know of the unnecessary ambiguities in the law and the frequently irrational and contrary findings of the courts. This calculated unpredictability provides a handsome living for lawyers while causing a huge amount of needless suffering for clients. Lawyers seem to be infiltrating and living comfortably in every nook and cranny of modern life. (Divorce lawyers are an egregious example.) In my opinion, the profession should be placed under the strict ethical control of non-lawyers.

Biotechnology

Massive public concern has been expressed over the genetic engineering of animals and crops and the production of human clones and 'designer' babies. Much of this debate has been ill-informed and based upon a knee-jerk dislike of 'interfering with nature'. Yet much in nature is already cruel and oppressive. It is, surely, morally desirable to alter nature in certain ways. Religious scruples seem irrational in this context. I can see no moral objection per se to cloning or to genetic engineering provided that (a) the production process itself entails no suffering, (b) that the transgenic or altered individuals so produced do not suffer increased pain or distress due to their altered natures, and (c) such products cause no more harm to others than do unaltered individuals.

Beside so many unnoticed cruelties in the world today, cloning seems to be morally insignificant.

Rule 41: The public needs to be fully informed about bio-technical developments. Bio-science and industry must be firmly regulated and controlled by agencies sensitive to public opinion that are entirely and demonstrably independent of commerce.

One of the really exciting prospects for genetic engineering, morally speaking, is its potential to *reduce the capacity for pain*. If, for example, it becomes possible to produce people and animals with reduced painience then this should be welcomed. What a revolution this will be! Ultimately there is the prospect of a painless future! Of course, there will be dangers. The trick will be to produce individuals who are largely analgesic but who are of no danger to themselves or others. So they will have to learn how to avoid being harmed even if they can feel no (severe) pain. They will, one hopes, still be able to feel joy and compassion and to show a moral concern for others. This will be a great challenge for science and for those ethical and democratic structures that control science.

International corporations and quangos

Globalism raises new moral problems, not least those caused by the increasing power of international bodies over our everyday lives. There is a need for international law to be developed so that the individual is as protected against the immoral actions of international corporations and institutions as he or she is protected against local bodies and governments by good domestic law.

The World Trade Organisation (WTO) seems to me a glaring example of power without moral responsibility. The only object of the WTO is to encourage world free trade. Few moral considerations are admitted into its decision-making procedures. Yet its decisions can, to a great extent, overrule the sovereignty of nations and even of major trading blocks such as the European Union.

There is an urgent need to reform the constitution of the WTO so that moral considerations concerning human rights (especially those concerned with the conditions of employment), the protection of the environment and the welfare of animals can be accepted as grounds for restrictions upon trade. The WTO must take into account the suffering of individuals. It must become ethical.

Computer technology

The computer or information technology revolution of the 1990s is causing considerably increased stress for many. By increasing the difficulties of everyday life, through the complications and frustrations of technology, increased de-personalisation and by flooding individuals with far more information than is required for balanced judgements to be made, it is damaging the quality of life for many people and so raises some ethical issues. Some people undoubtedly enjoy the new gadgetry and, if mastered, it can become an antidote to the boredom inherent in some jobs. But for others it is bewildering and has the dangerous effect of concentrating minds upon means rather than ends. There is little control over the quality and reliability of the information being made available on the internet. Every sort of crank and crackpot can disseminate junk disguised as fact. Applied ethics should be about ends – that is to say the consequences of actions in terms of their algesic effects upon others. Computer technology, if it becomes an end in itself, can distract us from what is really important. It can, too, become an aid to the invasion of privacy. Along with other electronic technology, such as the siting of closed circuit television cameras in almost every street in Britain, computers allow our private lives and identities to become the property of the regulatory authorities. The state will always have access to the best computers. Modern electronic technology poses a threat to civil liberties.

Environmental protection

The expansion of the environmental protection movement, along with animal rights, nuclear disarmament, the civil rights movement and the liberation of women, goes back to the social revolution of the 1960s. It coincides, too, with the developing interest in applied ethics. Environmentalism is based mainly upon a concern for the welfare of human beings, although this anthropocentric basis is sometimes concealed behind an expressed concern for the biosphere, the conservation of species or the protection of mountains, rivers, air or sea. Unlike, for example, the animal rights movement which expresses a concern for the well-being of individual animals per se, the environmental attitude is usually concerned to protect aspects of the environment for the benefit of humans. Elsewhere, I have suggested that there are at least seven motives for environmentalism. These seven motives or outlooks are the *thrifty*, the *aesthetic*, the *scientific*, the *historic*, the *health-conscious*, the *mystical* and the *compassionate*. Only the last two fully qualify in the requirement that morality must be about the well-being of *others*. The first five motives are rather more selfish, being anthropocentric concerns based upon preserving the environment for our future use scientifically or commercially, or for our health, or for our historic interest or aesthetic pleasure.[10] Of course, the well-being of human beings other than myself is of great moral importance. So, although non-painient things such as rivers and mountains can have no rights of their own, they are still morally important *indirectly*. The preservation of a beautiful mountain is, therefore, important because its destruction would cause aesthetic pain to many humans and also, presumably, because this would cause other sorts of pain to those animals who need it as a habitat. Painism focuses upon individuals and individual suffering whereas environmentalism considers other, more secondary values such as usefulness (e.g., biodiversity), hygiene and aesthetics, and is concerned with the conservation of species. Painism sometimes comes into conflict with environmentalism when the latter overlooks the suffering of individual painients. Also, there is a strange tendency for some environmentalists to take an ethnocentric view, favouring the extermination, for example, of species of plants and animals that are deemed to be 'foreign'. If this was to be applied in the human context it would be branded, rightly, as 'racism' or 'fascism'. This attitude is both irrational and, where it is applied to painient individuals, unethical.

Art and aesthetics

The concept of 'beauty' has become immensely unfashionable. Yet the popular culture of the twenty-first century gives pride of place to physically beautiful people and, to a lesser extent, to physically beautiful places. Perhaps because it is difficult to reproduce beauty the concept has almost disappeared from art. After Picasso, art became increasingly the cult of the ugly. Shock and disgust are emotional reactions that are so much easier to stimulate than aesthetic joy. Furthermore, they grab the attention of a jaded public. However, the real essentials of art are skill, beauty and imagination. Yet, for these qualities to be manifested, both talent and hard work are needed on the part of the artist. So these qualities, too, have become unfashionable. Aesthetics is about a form of pleasure, the psychological origins of which probably lie in sexual attraction. The deliberate creation of ugly things – in modern music, art and architecture, can cause slight but unnecessary pain. There is a minor duty, therefore, upon architects, artists, musicians, landscape gardeners and others to try to produce things of beauty. This does not mean, of course, that other qualities in contemporary art – its functionalism, fashionableness or fatuity, for example, are not good in themselves, provided they give pleasure and cause no pain.

Disgust is an emotion that is at last beginning to be studied. Disgust, although coloured by local culture, has a universal quality. In all human cultures, apparently, human faeces and urine, for example, are regarded with disgust. Yet nonhumans scarcely show this reaction towards excrement. If there is survival value in avoiding blood, vomit, disease, injury and faeces (which may well be the case because such things can certainly involve infection) then why do animals not avoid them? In fact, in the wild, animals do not contaminate themselves as much as they do in captivity.

Human infants do not show disgust until they are a few years old. Perhaps it is a learned behaviour or perhaps it manifests spontaneously at a certain critical age. Research will clarify this in due course. Disgust is akin to, but not quite the same as, what I have elsewhere called squeamishness (i.e., horror at the sight of injury or blood).[11] Both are powerful and unpleasant feelings that can contribute to the formation of ethical standards. Thus, what is considered 'dirty' is often thought of as also being 'wrong'. The dislike of others' bodies, particularly if these are unwashed, diseased, ugly or smelly, seems to be a natural or innate feeling among adults. Perhaps this is why the sexual drive needs to be so strong – it has to overcome such natural feelings of disgust. The olfactory sense is particularly powerful in triggering the emotions of disgust and squeamishness. Often these feelings are in direct opposition to our natural impulse of compassion which is, in my view, the engine of morality. Sometimes, however, squeamishness also points us in the same direction and away from causing deliberate damage to others.

Animal protection

The welfare of animals is a subject about which I have written extensively.[12] Indeed, my theories of speciesism and painism were originally developed in this context. The idea of speciesism emphasises that our conventional mistreatment of nonhuman animals in laboratories, farms, places of entertainment, our homes and in the wild, is based upon discrimination which is as irrational and evil as is racism, ageism or sexism. A difference in species is as morally irrelevant as are differences in race, age or gender. None of these differences justify moral discrimination. The morally crucial similarity between ourselves and the other animals is our capacity to suffer – our painience. From this flows the conclusion that whatever is right or wrong in our treatment of other human beings is also right or wrong in our treatment of painient individuals of other species, however small they may be. In other words, if we are going to be rational as well as compassionate, then we must apply our moral rules, whatever these are, equally to humans and nonhumans. This is a moral revolution. Of course, as painists we are concerned about the painful consequences of our actions and what is painful for one sort of individual is not necessarily painful for a different sort. So, taking away a cricket bat from a human child might well cause considerable suffering and so be wrong, whereas removing the bat from a camel is unlikely to have a similar effect. But suffering is suffering in whatever species it occurs. So X units of suffering in a camel, whatever the cause, are equally morally important as are X units of suffering in a human.

The revelation in 2001 that humans have only some 30,000 genes – not many more than other animals – surprised some people. But why should it? Our ability to talk, and transmit accumulated information, has led to a rapidly escalating *appearance* of difference between ourselves and other species. But for thousands of years, during the Old Stone Age, with the same number of genes, we hardly progressed at all. All the trappings of civilisation are but skin deep. We are all animals beneath the veneer.

Rule 42: Moral standards should apply equally to all painient individuals regardless of species.

Although there are differences between painients, the great similarity is our painience. There is growing scientific evidence that many nonhumans can suffer very much as humans do. Like us, they feel not only pain but also fear and boredom. Yet everywhere nonhumans remain our slaves.

The animal protection movement in Europe (although not the USA) has been highly effective in converting its ethical principles into law. Often we have led the way in methods of reform. In 1995, for example, I arranged the first meeting with NGOs that the Director General of the WTO had ever had, in an attempt to infuse a moral dimension into the operations of that powerful body.

The animal ethicists have also played a leading role in clarifying the discussion of consciousness. Marian Stamp Dawkins has mentioned half a dozen common pitfalls in discussion of the subject – viz., the confusion of the terms 'cognition' with 'consciousness', the different uses of the argument from analogy with ourselves, assuming that 'preference' necessarily implies consciousness, or that autonomic responses (heart rate, body temperature, hormone levels, etc.) do so, assuming that complexity of behaviour implies consciousness or that only complex organisms can be conscious.[13] Another very common confusion, I believe, is the assumption that consciousness means 'free will' or the capacity to make decisions. As I have pointed out, electrons and other subatomic particles, behave in an unpredictable manner as if they, too, have a mind of their own; yet I certainly would not suggest that they are conscious. For Immanuel Kant the central issue of philosophy is how morality and free will can exist in a world that is amenable to scientific explanation. If human behaviour is strictly determined we can have no moral choice over what actions we take. Kant concluded that there is, therefore, a nonscientific realm in which we make decisions. Kant, of course, accepted Newtonian science and its straightforward deterministic view of the universe. Today, however, we can find a place for 'free will' *within* the teachings of modern science and, especially, quantum mechanics.

From the point of view of ethics, qualities such as autonomy, self-consciousness, cognition, the abilities to use language or observe duties are all irrelevant. As I have argued, the only morally relevant quality is painience – the capacity to suffer pain or distress. In discussing animal welfare there are at least three concepts of welfare commonly used – (1) pain and pleasure, (2) health and fitness, or (3) the opportunity for animals to 'express their natures' (or *telos*).[14] Michael Appleby refers to these as emphasising animals' minds, bodies and natures respectively.[15] Obviously, it is of importance for veterinary surgeons to monitor health and fitness but from the ethical viewpoint it is again, only the first, the emphasis upon painience, that really matters. Health and fitness and the ability to 'express one's nature' are important because they *cause* pain and pleasure. An unhealthy animal is likely (eventually at least) to be a suffering animal. So, too, is an animal who is unable to express its nature – that is to say an animal whose drives, impulses and preferences are frustrated. All these points apply in human ethics also. Animals, whether human or nonhuman, have welfares. What matters morally about their welfares is their subjective experience of pains and pleasures. We have already concluded that pains are partly composed of 'direct' pains or the *pains of stimulation* (whether these are sensations, emotions or cognitions) and partly of the 'indirect' *pains of deprivation*. These are the two main sources of suffering. When gauging welfare it is not a question of one or the other, it is a question of taking both into account (and *see* pp. 53ff., above).

Humans have become accustomed to the idea that they have a right to exploit nonhumans for food, science and sport. Foxhunters, for example, claim that they are an oppressed minority whose rights are being crushed by animal welfare campaigners. But nobody can legitimately have a right to be cruel. There can no more be a right to cause pain to an animal in the pursuit of sporting pleasure than to cause pain to a woman or child in pursuit of sexual pleasure.

Some final thoughts on suffering

Often, in such discussions, there seem to be many words pursuing only a few ideas. Many different words really describe the same things. For example, 'well-being', 'quality of life' and 'welfare' are, for our purposes, synonymous, as are 'pain', 'suffering' and 'distress'. Also synonymous are 'happiness', 'the good life', 'contentment', *eudaimonia* and *ataraxia*. 'Living natural lives', 'expressing one's nature', 'the fulfilment of psychological needs', 'the satisfaction of desires or preferences' and even, perhaps, talk of *telos* are all about the same thing – the happiness that arises from the satisfaction of learned and unlearned drives. Behaviourism having been thrown out of the window (quite rightly), people seem to be forgetting what is known about behaviour. This is a pity. Perhaps the disciplines of experimental psychology and philosophy have been for too long apart. Michael Appleby points out that sometimes the satisfaction of preferences, desires or drives causes pleasure only when the individual is *aware* that there is satisfaction. A parent is only happy when she *knows* that her lost child is safe. But there are also cases where satisfaction can unconsciously cause conscious pleasure. We are often unaware of what is making us happy or sad and, of course, our desires are frequently unconscious. But, however interesting such issues are psychologically, all that matters morally is our conscious state. Appleby has suggested there may be 'no shared mental quality' between such painful states as nausea, intense physical pain, anxiety or those caused by the frustration of not being able to walk around. But surely – their *painfulness* is shared. Their causes may differ, and so do their emotional and cognitive attributes, but at some basic level these states are all painful. And this is precisely the quality that matters morally.[16]

One cannot distinguish meaningfully, as Appleby appears to try to do, between painful mental states and how much such states 'matter to the individual' mentally. 'Mattering' is a very important part of the painfulness of the mental state! When we talk of mattering we are, in this case, talking of suffering. Appleby concludes that a brief definition of (animal) welfare is not possible. But surely it is. Welfare means happiness. As simple as that. Much of the muddle seems to arise from the failure to distinguish between the two main causes of suffering – that is to say *direct* (e.g., a red hot iron) and *indirect* (i.e., the frustration of drives and desires). Suffering can be caused by one or other or by both. Just as surely as does a red hot iron, the failure to satisfy a drive or a preference or a desire always, per se, produces pain (suffering) in a conscious painient individual whether or not they are aware of the actual cause. To the moralist it is only their awareness of the pain, and not of its cause, that matters.

This discussion also raises the question: are pain and pleasure the opposite ends of the same dimension or are they two separate systems? I think they are probably both. That is to say at a deep level physiologically (sub-cortically), they are on the same dimension so that they can compete and conflict. (Pains, as I have suggested, tend to dominate pleasures.) But more superficially (cortically) they are clearly separate systems. The pleasures of playing golf while listening to Verdi on my headset are obviously two separate pleasures cognitively, just as the pain of my bunion and the thought of next week's visit to the mother-in-law are separate pains. Similarly, pains and pleasures, too, can be seen as separate systems. Their cognitive components, for example, are entirely distinct. Fraser and Duncan[17] have asked whether indirect pains and pleasures are the *results* of drive and drive-satiation respectively or do they themselves *drive* behaviour? Is sexual attraction (clearly a drive) also itself pleasurable? Possibly, yes. But is hunger (clearly a drive) also itself a pleasure? Probably not. The answers are not entirely easy. Also, the human animal can fantasise pleasures. Imagining sexual intercourse or a well-prepared meal are pleasurable imaginings. Some behaviours are motivated by the avoidance of pain (e.g., by the satiation of drives) and some, apparently, by the search for direct pleasures e.g., going to the opera or lying in the sun. The drive mechanisms and the reward mechanisms, however, seem to be separate. Moreover, when hunger drives me to eat I seem to be deriving reward from two separate systems – i) the reduction of painful hunger drive, and ii) the pleasurable taste of food. When my hunger is entirely satiated I can still derive pleasure from the second system – the taste of the food. But eating when hungry is often regarded as being more pleasurable. Why is this? Is the reduction of hunger drive itself a pleasure or does hunger intensify the pleasures of the second system – the taste system? Again, I think it may be both. Other drives seem to operate similarly. The satiation of sexual drive is itself a form of pleasure – the pleasure of relief. But it is *also* a direct pleasure, involving pleasurable sensations. Clearly, the mechanisms are complex and drives differ slightly one from another. However, I think we can assert that the reduction of painful drive states can do more than reduce pain: they can also produce actual pleasure. Quenching thirst, for example, is itself pleasurable. Fraser and Duncan conclude that whereas painful states have evolved to meet serious survival threats (e.g., threats of attack or threats to reproductive success), pleasurable states have evolved in 'opportunity situations' where the threat to survival is low. If this is so, it is another instance of the greater biological importance of pain over pleasure.

How can one test such hypotheses? The human animal can give subjective reports. But are there any *objective* indices of pain and pleasure? Objective changes such as the autonomic effects of stress (alterations in heart rate, respiration, blood pressure, hormone levels, galvanic skin response and so on) are rather non-specific. That is to say that they occur in any arousal situation whether it is painful or pleasurable. This is important to know. There is, as yet, no easy way to distinguish and measure levels of pain or pleasure physiologically – although two possible avenues should be explored – first, the use of brain scans and, secondly, the measurement of brain opioids, pain transmitters and other neurotransmitters such as serotonin. If animals can tell us through their behaviour which situations they prefer, and these preferences can be ranked, then it should be possible to look for correlates between preferences and these two sorts of measures.

What is the relevance of all this to ethics? Well, if pain (suffering) is the central criterion of ethics, as I have claimed, then it would help us to measure the rightness and wrongness of situations if we could *objectively* measure their pain content. This would be particularly helpful when we are dealing with individuals who can neither tell us about their experiences nor indicate their preferences through their behaviour. Basically, we should try to do to them what we would like done to us.

Conclusion

I admit that I have sometimes allowed my irritation to show at what I consider to be the ethical inconsistencies and the odd moral priorities of our society. If this book is anything, it is a plug for compassion to be shown to every suffering individual. Our empathy with others is a vital human characteristic. It is innate and powerful and probably a spill-over of our great capacity for altruism as parents. Compassion is often triggered and directed by our experiences with the suitable objects of such feeling, whether these are human or nonhuman.[18]

In this chapter I have tried to apply the principles of painism (as previously outlined in chapter 2) to various practical problems. In doing so, I may have failed in some cases, usually because we lack the information to predict and measure accurately the painful consequences of our actions. In these and other cases I may simply appear opinionated. Several lessons, however, can be learned. If painism is applied to our everyday experiences it can clarify our moral decision-making by concentrating our minds not upon secondary principles such as equality, liberty or democracy but upon the *suffering* of others, and by focusing not upon how many sufferers there are but upon the severity of the suffering of individuals. *It is the quantity of individual suffering that matters and not the quantity of sufferers.*

It is my sincere hope that this chapter has also introduced a few new topics into applied ethics and challenged the ethical importance attached conventionally to others.

References

Chapter 1

[1] Richard D. Ryder, *Animal Revolution: Changing Attitudes Towards Speciesism*, Basil Blackwell, Oxford, 1989; rev. ed. Berg, Oxford, 2000

[2] James Rachels, *The Elements of Moral Philosophy*, Random House, New York, 1986

[3] J. L. Mackie, *Ethics: Inventing Right and Wrong*, Penguin Books, Harmondsworth, 1990

[4] G. E. Moore, *Principia Ethica*, 1903

[5] Thomas Nagel, *The Possibility of Altruism*, Princeton University Press, Princeton, NJ, 1991

[6] R. B. Brandt, *A Theory of the Good and the Right*, Clarendon Press, Oxford, 1979

[7] Richard D. Ryder, *Speciesism*, privately printed in Oxford, 1970; and Richard D. Ryder, chapter I, *Animals Men and Morals*, Godlovitch and Harris, eds., Gollancz, London, 1971

[8] Ayn Rand, *The Virtue of Selfishness*, Princeton University Press, Princeton, NJ, 1965

[9] Brenda Almond, in a review of Peter Singer's *Animal Liberation* in the *New York Review of Books*, 1975

[10] Robert Nozick, *Anarchy, State & Utopia*, Basil Books, New York, 1974

[11] Ronald Dworkin, *Taking Rights Seriously*, Duckworth, London, 1978

[12] Peter Singer, 'Ethics', *Encyclopedia Britannica*, p. 514

[12] Peter Singer, 'Animal Liberation', *New York Review of Books*, New York NY, 1975

[13] Peter Singer, *Practical Ethics*, Cambridge University Press, Cambridge, 1979

[14] Thomas Mautner, *A Dictionary of Philosophy*, Blackwell, Oxford, 1996

Chapter 2

[1] *See* Richard D. Ryder, 'Painism: Some Moral Rules for the Civilized Experimenter', *Cambridge Quarterly of Healthcare Ethics*, vol. 8, 1, 1999.

[2] Patrick Wall, *Pain: The Science of Suffering*, Weidenfield and Nicolson, London, 1999

[3] Jeremy Bentham, *An Introduction to the Principles of Morals and Legislation*, 1789, chap. 1, section 3

[4] In an editorial in *The Economist*, 18 December 1999

[5] Steven Pinker, *How the Mind Works*, Penguin Books, Harmondsworth, 1997, p. 392

[6] Roger Scruton, *On Hunting*, Yellow Jersey Press, London, 1998

[7] Richard D. Ryder, various leaflets e.g., *Speciesism: The Ethics of Vivisection*, Scottish Society for the Prevention of Vivisection, Edinburgh, 1974

[8] Jonathan Glover, *Causing Death and Saving Lives*, Pelican Books, Harmondsworth, 1977

[9] Joseph Fletcher, *Situation Ethics: The New Morality*, John Knox Press, Louiseville, KY, 1966

[10] Richard D. Ryder, letters published in the *Daily Telegraph*, 'Rights of Non Human Animals', 7 April 1969, 3 May 1969 and 20 May 1969

[11] Richard D. Ryder, Introduction in Ryder, ed., *Animal Welfare and the Environment*, Duckworth, London, 1992

[12] J. Baird Callicott, 'Animal Liberation: A Triangular Affair', in *In Defense of the Land Ethic,* State University of New York Press, Albany, NY, 1989

[13] Richard D. Ryder, chap. , in Godlovitch and Harris (eds.), *Animals Men and Morals*, Gollancz, London, 1971; Peter Singer, 'Animal Liberation', *New York Review of Books*, 1975; Tom Regan, *The Case for Animal Rights*, University of California Press, Berkeley, CA, 1984

[14] Richard D. Ryder, 'Painism' in Ruth Chadwick, ed., *Encyclopedia of Applied Ethics*, vol. 3, Academic Press, San Diego, CA, 1998

[15] Peter Singer, *The Ethics of Animal Liberation – A Summary,* RSPCA leaflet, 1993

[16] Tom Regan, *The Rights View,* RSPCA leaflet, 1993

[17] Personal Communications to the author, 1999

[18] Tom Regan, *The Case for Animal Rights*, University of California Press, CA, 1984

[19] Benjamin Libet, 'Neural time factors in conscious and unconscious mental functions', in *Towards a Sceince of Consciousness*, S. R. Hameroff *et al* (eds), MIT Press, Cambridge, MA, 1996, pp. 337–47.

[20] Robert Melzack. 'Pain', no. 1 of the McGill pain questionnaire, McGill University, McGill, NV, 1975

[21] Robert Melzack and P. D. Wall, *The Challenge of Pain*, Penguin Books, Harmondsworth, 1982

[22] Richard D. Ryder, 'Painism: Historical and Ethical Aspects', paper delivered at the Symposium *The Science and Philosophy of Pain*, Viaams Diergeneeskundig Tijdschrift, Ghent, 2000, 69, pp. 401–06

[23] Robert Wright, *The Moral Animal: Why We Are the Way We Are*, Pantheon, New York, 1994; Abacus, London, 1997

[24] George C. Williams, *Adaptation and Natural Selection: A Critique of Some Current Evolutionary Thought*, Princeton University Press, Princeton, NJ, 1966 (*see also* Robert Trivers, 'The Evolution of Reciprocal Altruism', *Quarterly Review of Biology*, 1971, 46, pp. 35–6

[25] Robert Wright, *The Moral Animal: Why We Are the Way We Are*, Pantheon, New York, 1994; Abacus, London, 1997

Chapter 3

[1] *Daily Telegraph*, 12 August 2000 and 'Family Man is Destroyed by Sex with a Girl 20 Years Ago', *Daily Express*, 11 January 2001

[2] 'How a Boy of 14 Carried Housewife to Bed over his Shoulder', *Daily Mail*, 27 September 2000, p. 5. *See also* 'Wife Seduced Boy, 13', *Daily Mail*, 27 March 2000.

[3] John Rawls, *A Theory of Justice*, Harvard University Press, Cambridge, MA. 1971

[4] Ronald Dworkin, *Sovereign Virtue: The Theory and Practice of Equality,* Harvard University Press, Cambridge, MA, 2000

[5] John Stuart Mill, 'On Liberty', in Mary Warnock (ed.) *Utilitarianism and Other Writings,* Collins, Glasgow, 1962

[6] Peter Singer, 'A New Ethics' in Sian Griffiths (ed.) *Predictions: 30 Great Minds on the Future*, Oxford University Press, Oxford, 1999

[7] Jonathan Glover, *Causing Death and Saving Lives*, Pelican Books, Harmondsworth, 1977

[8] A. J. Coates, *The Ethics of War*, Manchester University Press, Manchester, 1997

[9] *Human Rights*, London, HMSO, 1995

[10] Richard D. Ryder (ed.) *Animal Welfare and the Environment*, Duckworth, London, 1992

[11] Richard D. Ryder, *Victims of Science: The Use of Animals in Research*, Davis-Poynter, London, 1975; revised edition, Centaur Press, London, 1980

[12] Richard D. Ryder, *Animal Revolution: Changing Attitudes Towards Speciesism*, Blackwell, Oxford, 1989; rev. ed., Berg, Oxford, 2000; idem, *The Political Animal: The Conquest of Speciesism*, McFarland, 1998

[13] Marian Stamp Dawkins, *Who Needs Consciousness?*, UFAW Conference, London, 2000

[14] I. J. H. Duncan and D. Fraser, 'Understanding Animal Welfare' in M. C. Appleby and B. O. Hughes (eds.) *Animal Welfare*, CAB International, Wallingford, 1997

[15] M.C. Appleby, *Tower of Babel: Variation in Ethical Approaches, Concepts of Welfare and Attitudes to Genetic Manipulation* in *Animal Welfare*, 8, 1999, pp. 381–90

[16] M. C. Appleby and P. Sandoe, 'Philosophical Debates Relevant to Animal Welfare: The Nature of Well-being', article submitted to *Animal Welfare*, 2000

[17] D. Fraser and I. J. H. Duncan, 'Pleasures, Pains and Animal Welfare', in *Animal Welfare*, vol. 7, 4, 1998

[18] Elizabeth S. Paul, 'Empathy with Animals and with Humans: Are they Linked?', *Anthrozoos*, 13, 4, 2000, pp. 194–203.

Index